A GRIZZLY IN THE MAIL AND OTHER ADVENTURES IN AMERICAN HISTORY

Tim Grove

University of Nebraska Press | Lincoln and London

Library of Congress Cataloging-in-Publication Data
Grove, Tim, 1967–
A grizzly in the mail and other adventures
in American history / Tim Grove.
pages   cm
Includes bibliographical references.
ISBN 978-0-8032-4972-1 (pbk.: alk. paper) —
ISBN 978-0-8032-5405-3 (epub) —
ISBN 978-0-8032-5406-0 (mobi) —
ISBN 978-0-8032-5404-6 (pdf)
1. United States—History—Anecdotes. 2. United
States—Biography—Anecdotes. I. Title.
E179.G84 2014
973—dc23
2013039704

Set in Lyon by Laura Wellington.

For my parents

Remember the days of old; consider the generations long past. Ask your father and he will tell you, your elders, and they will explain to you.

—*Deuteronomy 32:7*

CONTENTS

INTRODUCTION

> History is not about dates and quotes and obscure
> provisos. History is about life, about change, about
> consequences, cause and effect. It's about the
> mystery of human nature, the mystery of time,
> and it isn't just about politics and the military and
> social issues, which is almost always the way it's
> taught. It's about music and poetry and drama
> and science and medicine and money and love.
>
> —*David McCullough*

My friend Siobhan says history is gossip on a grand scale. John F. Kennedy wrote that "for the true student of history—history is an end in itself. It fulfills a deep human need for understanding; the satisfaction it provides requires no further justification." I've found that people either proclaim they love history or hate it. History enthusiasts consider the study of history endlessly fascinating while others find it deadly dull. Some people stand on a historic battlefield and see only a grassy field while others see military strategy and the chaos of war. What are the components that make history engaging and compelling? What does it mean to experience history?

For over twenty years my goal has been to help history haters change their minds. I have managed to mold my passion for history into a profession pursuing intriguing stories from the past and sharing them with millions of people.

What do riding a high wheel bicycle, ginning cotton, harnessing a mule, pursuing buffalo, finding an Amishman, flying over the Hell Stretch, dancing a Native dance, and tracking down a grizzly have in common? I've undertaken these tasks in part because of work projects, but mostly for the sheer love of history. My eclectic adventures have given me insight into the breadth of American history and its intrigues. Now I can really understand the impact of the so-called safety bicycle's invention because I have tried to ride its predecessor, the high wheeler. History should be about active pursuit.

When I first sat down at my desk in the restored James Anderson House at Colonial Williamsburg one summer as a determined graduate intern, I embarked on a history career that would take me on a rewarding journey behind the scenes at the most popular history museums in America.

This book chronicles my personal pilgrimage into the past, a journey that I haven't yet completed. The chapters follow my career beginning with a graduate internship at Colonial Williamsburg, one of the nation's largest outdoor history sites. Williamsburg is a carefully cultivated immersive environment that sweeps visitors into another time. It's a place that inspired my love of history and challenged me to consider what it means to experience the past. The Smithsonian's National Portrait Gallery, where I presented student programs, provided an excellent foundation for a budding historian. In its corridors of faces I began to see the necessity of thinking about the past from multiple perspectives. At the Smithsonian's National Museum of American History I delved into historical research, looking at primary sources and actively engaging with the past. I touched history with my bare hands and enjoyed every moment. In a three-year stint at the Missouri Historical Society I developed a national traveling exhibition and gained valuable insight into other cultures. My travels out west opened my eyes to the power of place. At the Smithsonian's National Air and Space Museum I learned how to humanize the past and to make historical topics engaging and compelling.

The stories and reflections in this book show that history is not the boring subject of a childhood classroom but a rich and profound exploration of the tapestry of life. We can understand ourselves better when we start to make sense of those who came before us, the challenges they faced, and the decisions they made. In these pages you will meet both famous and unfamiliar characters from the past and gain new understandings of a variety of historical subjects, like the cotton gin and the Star-Spangled Banner. By following along on my historical encounters I hope you will either find a renewed interest in the past or realize that history is indeed anything but boring.

1
WHY HISTORY?

A morsel of genuine history is a thing
so rare as to be always valuable.

—*Thomas Jefferson to John Adams, 1817*

One typically hot summer day in Williamsburg, Virginia, I noticed
a crowd of people gathering on the lawn of the Governor's Palace.
Their darting glances and excited chatter hinted at something great
about to happen. Eavesdropping on various conversations, I quickly
learned that His Excellency Governor Thomas Jefferson was scheduled to arrive at any moment to address the assembly.

Sure enough, the governor soon appeared in a dark suit with white
silk stockings, red hair pulled back in a queue. He stepped to the
podium and gave a brief address, providing details about the seat
of government's move to Richmond and an update on the progress
of the war. He then graciously offered to answer questions.

Some audience members asked prepared questions related to the
governor's talk, while others seized the opportunity to inquire about
more personal topics. At times the governor seemed unclear about

a question, alternating between caution and confidence. Typical of most politicians, he provided carefully worded responses that only sometimes held an answer. But he maintained a dignity that one would expect. After a dozen or so questions, his aides signaled it was time to end. He bid *adieu* and walked back into the Palace.

This innovative program brought about by twentieth-century historians was an experiment, an attempt to provoke deeper thinking. A departure from Colonial Williamsburg's usual re-creation of historical events, it sought to take visitors back to the eighteenth century along with some familiar, modern-day constructs. In other words, the press conference—common today, but unheard of in the 1700s—creatively merged the two time periods for the benefit of today's audience.

The staff at Williamsburg and other history sites wants visitors to "experience" history. What does this mean? One can visit Yosemite National Park and experience the beauty and grandeur of nature. One can go whitewater rafting and experience the rush of the river and the cold wetness of the water as it splashes the face. But experiencing history? Do you experience history when you walk the hallowed ground of a battlefield or visit a historical house? Experience in verb form implies action. What action is actually taking place?

The success of the press conference and similar presentations relies on an audience's suspension of disbelief and willingness to go along with the role play of time travel. As audience members at the press conference, visitors could ask a prepared question or one of their own. They could be as active as they chose or silently absorb the unfolding event. During the program, they learned that Thomas Jefferson, as the second governor of the state of Virginia, had lived in the Palace prior to the capital's move to Richmond and had succeeded Patrick Henry, Virginia's first governor. As I stood there watching the program that day, I observed the people in the audience. What were they thinking? They seemed fully engaged, the concept alien yet familiar enough to captivate them.

It only takes a spark to kindle the fire of a lifelong learner. That is teaching. As Anatole France said, "Awaken people's curiosity. It is enough to open their mind, do not overload them. Put there just a spark."

Origins of a History Geek

What was the spark in my childhood that captured a young boy's imagination and triggered a historical curiosity that would last a lifetime? How did I become a history geek? Was it dressing up in knee breeches and stockings, making beeswax candles and sewing a braided rug to celebrate America's bicentennial in elementary school? Was it the numerous childhood family vacations to historic sites—Monticello, Gettysburg, Bunker Hill, Hyde Park? Or is it carried in the genes, inherited from my father, the reader of the family?

Perhaps it was listening to my grandmother tell stories of her childhood. I vividly remember one about her riding home in a sleigh, tucked under a pile of blankets to keep warm, and somehow getting dumped out into a huge snowdrift and laughing about it. My mind could not imagine a world so idyllic. Even at a young age I realized the incredible inventions my grandparents had watched become a part of everyday life. Born just before the turn of the twentieth century, my grandmother could remember a childhood rhyme about the assassin of President Garfield. She saw the birth of the airplane, the family car, and radio and television and air conditioning. My child's mind could barely comprehend a life without these everyday items, a world where the everyday was so different.

Primed by the excitement of the nation's bicentennial, my nascent fascination with history blossomed. During a few summers in my childhood I spent a week in the Poconos at my aunt and uncle's house. They served on the board of the Wayne County Historical Society, where they volunteered each week. I would go along and explore the aisles of dusty artifacts. Coal was the main product of the region, and one year they celebrated the sesquicentennial of the area's biggest claim to fame, the Stourbridge Lion, the first locomotive to operate in the Western Hemisphere. Its trial run in

1829 had launched a new era in commercial transportation and the celebration of the anniversary focused on a full-scale replica of the Lion owned by the Historical Society. The event inspired my inner poet and I wrote a poem about the Lion, sold trinkets related to the event at the historical society, and rode a steam train. I had no idea that I would one day work in the National Museum of American History, which owns the Lion's main boiler and several other parts of the engine.

And then there was the family reunion. One summer we traveled to the Shenandoah Valley in Virginia and took a tour of sites associated with our family history. One tale captured my imagination. We were standing in the kitchen of an old farmhouse. Our guide, well versed in family lore, pointed out the large brick fireplace and stated that during the Civil War my great-great-grandfather wanted to ensure that his family was provided for, should something happen to him. He removed a brick from the fireplace, inserted one hundred gold coins, and carefully replaced the brick. He wanted to make certain the Yankees would not find the money. When the war ended, he gave each of his three sons one of the coins. Today only one of the coins' whereabouts is known and, ironically, much to the chagrin of our Southern family members, it's in Yankee hands. My grandfather moved north to Pennsylvania and eventually gave the coin to my father, who is a native Pennsylvanian. The small USA coin, about the size of a dime, has Lady Liberty's face on the front. Whenever I look at it, I imagine the hands it has touched, the pockets and money purses it has seen, and the items it has purchased.

A few years after the reunion I read about a grand finale to the national celebration of America's bicentennial to take place in Yorktown, Virginia. With President Ronald Reagan and French President François Mitterrand in attendance, it would be a huge reenactment of the surrender of British general Charles Cornwallis to Gen. George Washington. I begged my parents to take me and we braved the crowds to witness the spectacle. As muffled drums beat a steady march and fifes played "The World Turned Upside

Down," my young mind imagined the autumn day that sent shock waves through the British government. The stunned British troops, colors cased, laid down their arms, essentially ending the American Revolution. As I explored the rows of Continental soldier tents and talked to the reenactors, I could not contain my excitement. A history spark deep within had caught fire and the flame was growing.

A Place of Inspiration

While I can't pinpoint a moment, I can identify a place that greatly contributed to my love of history. This place, like few others in America, has the power to foster a fascination for history: the restored colonial capital of Virginia, Williamsburg.

Turning off interstate 64 heading east from Richmond, a traveler passes through thick forests edging tidal creeks. Tucked away in Virginia's tidewater region is America's largest outdoor history museum, a restored town brought to life every day of the year by hundreds of costumed interpreters who face the daunting challenge of transporting visitors back in time to the eighteenth century, when America declared her independence from Great Britain.

The restoration of the town began in 1926 through the generosity of millionaire John D. Rockefeller Jr., whose money transformed the faded, sleepy Southern town into a jewel of historic preservation. Today Colonial Williamsburg, the popular name of the restoration and foundation that runs it, exemplifies history immersion.

If the easiest way to learn a language is immersion, surrounding oneself with native speakers, then perhaps the same could be said of history. Colonial Williamsburg douses its visitors in the sights, sounds, smells, tastes, and feel of life in the 1770s. Walking the Williamsburg streets seems the equivalent of entering a foreign country. At once the visitor grabs on to the recognizable while engulfed in a sea of the unfamiliar. From the *clip-clop* of horse-drawn carriages to the high-pitched shrill of fifes and the boom of cannons, the sounds of long-ago life assault the ears. Intricately carved wood paneling, neatly clipped boxwoods, unusual brick patterns, gun smoke, gingerbread, ink, wood, leather, horse dung, peanut soup—all blend together into a feast for the senses.

Into this alternate universe walked a ten-year-old boy who has not been the same since. Several decades ago, I stood transfixed by this captivating world. The colonial music teacher demonstrated an eighteenth-century hunting horn for me, a budding French horn player. I marveled at the sight of food prepared on an open spit. The far-off sounds of the fife and drum corps called me to watch their procession down the street, my excitement building as boys my own age marched out of a distant time past.

A sense of curiosity about that past gripped me and has yet to let go. The inspiration from my first several visits prompted me to read every book about Williamsburg that I could get my hands on.

As I grew older this fascination led to the dream and then the actual quest for a job at Colonial Williamsburg. I graduated from college, not with a history degree but a journalism degree, with emphasis in public relations. I had considered a history degree but had no interest in teaching in a classroom and had yet to consider the multitude of other options available to history majors. Therefore it seemed logical to look for a job in public relations at a history museum—not just any history museum, but Colonial Williamsburg.

In the years following graduation I called the jobs hotline at Williamsburg month after month, hoping there would be a position suited to my skills. When a PR opening was finally advertised, I wracked my brain to figure out how to get noticed among the myriad candidates. Then an idea hit! I went to work with the help of my cousin and her husband. On yellow parchment paper we carefully crafted a letter of recommendation from the past. My hometown, Lancaster, Pennsylvania, had also been home to one of the signers of the Declaration of Independence, George Ross. In neat script, "Mr. Ross" highly recommended my PR skills to the Department of Human Resources at Colonial Williamsburg and signed the letter with a flourish. The letter was carefully folded, sealed with a blob of red wax, and sent via Federal Express. I waited and waited for an invitation to interview for the position. I never received one, although a friendly man in HR actually phoned to acknowledge my creativity. Still, I was crushed.

Several years later, after career counseling and enlightenment about the field of public history—the use of history skills in a non-academic setting—I enrolled in the graduate history program at George Mason University outside of Washington DC. The program required six credit hours of work at a history museum, and I knew that Williamsburg had an internship program. This could be my opportunity. No one from my graduate program had interned at Williamsburg before, but a classmate directed me to a friend who had just completed an internship at Williamsburg and could give me a connection. I guess I called the right person because, to my relief, he had a project for me and offered me a summer internship. At last it seemed the door was opening.

In late May of 1992, I packed the car and drove two and half hours south. I arrived in Williamsburg not knowing a soul, with no place to stay, and with very few details about my internship or leads for a part-time paying job. I would be working for an office called Interpretive Development—a mysterious but compelling name. I wasn't really sure what it meant. But I didn't care because I would have almost three months to explore the inner workings of this place, to watch visitors engage with history, and to attempt to understand why they came.

Mysterious Passions

Why history? Why do some people love the past while others are enthralled with the future or can't get enough of Tolkien's Middle-earth? Why does science fiction hold so little interest for me, while historical fiction engages me? Who can say why people are drawn to machines, or medicine, or animals, or ideas? Rarely can we clearly identify the sources of our passions. It is actually easier to state why we dislike something.

I suspect those who claim to dislike history have never truly encountered the past in a way that captivated their imagination. To me, history requires a great deal of imagination, and mine revs up when I start looking at primary source materials and begin asking questions. The study of history has often been compared with detective work. Both require the practitioner to make hypotheses and inferences, to think critically and to draw firm conclusions based on the evidence at hand. When the rote facts of history give way to multiple perspectives, conflicting opinions, and sometimes even mysteries, my mind is engaged and my curiosity piqued.

Many history educators fail to convey why the discipline of history is relevant and how the past informs the present. Novelist and social critic James Baldwin wrote, "History does not refer merely, or even principally, to the past. On the contrary, the great force of history comes from the fact that we carry it within us, are unconsciously controlled by it in many ways, and history is literally *present* in all that we do."

President John F. Kennedy was an avid student of history, and in 1962 the editors of *American Heritage* magazine asked him to reflect on why knowing history is important. He wrote an impassioned essay beginning with this sentence: "There is little that is more important for an American citizen to know than the history and traditions of his country." He went on to justify the study of history, beginning with the fact that it is a pleasure for its own sake. He wrote, "The American past is a record of stirring achievement in the face of stubborn difficulty. It is a record filled with figures larger than life, with high drama and hard decision, with valor and with tragedy, with incidents both poignant and picturesque, and with the excitement and hope involved in the conquest of a wilderness and the settlement of a continent. For the true historian—and for the true student of history—history is an end in itself. It fulfills a deep human need for understanding; the satisfaction it provides requires no further justification."

When I began my internship at Williamsburg I wasn't sure what path my career would take. I only knew that I found the study of history deeply satisfying. What were my expectations? I was convinced this would be the best summer of my life. I was sure some form of history career was my destiny. With such high hopes, I prepared to seize the opportunity and take advantage of every moment. I gazed through rose-tinted glasses at one of the largest history organizations in the country. Would experience match expectation?

2
STEPPING BACK IN TIME, ALMOST

What we shall some day become will grow
inexorably out of what today we are; and what
we are now, in its turn, comes out of what earlier
Americans were—out of what they did and
thought and dreamed and hoped for, out of their
trials and their aspirations, out of their shining
victories and their dark and tragic defeats.

—*Historian Bruce Catton, from an address
on the "Lost Colony," 1958*

When people find out I worked at Colonial Williamsburg, their first
question is usually "Did you dress up?" At some point early in the
foundation's history, the management decided to populate the restored town with staff dressed in eighteenth-century clothing—and
today a visitor to Williamsburg can encounter hundreds of costumed employees. While early staff members were local women

serving as tour guides or "hostesses," today several kinds of costumed employees work in the historic area. Some actually portray historic characters—based on real people from the past—and speak in first-person present tense as if they live in the eighteenth century.

A visitor to Colonial Williamsburg may converse with George and Martha Washington, Thomas Jefferson, George Wythe, Patrick Henry, Peyton Randolph, and many other residents of or travelers to the eighteenth-century town. This approach, termed "living history" by its proponents, is used by various outdoor museums around the world. Other museums in the United States that practice living history include Old Sturbridge Village and Plimoth Plantation in Massachusetts, and Conner Prairie in Indiana. Williamsburg is considered a leader in this method. The technique of living history is intended to help immerse visitors in the past and provide a more personal approach, but the practice has its share of critics. As one museum professional put it, "The teaching approach [living history] is praised for the extensive historical research it often requires but damned as frivolous show-business entertainment."

A well-presented living history program can transport the visitor to another time period and teach history in a way that can be very effective. A quality program requires rigorous training for the staff. A character interpreter must feel comfortable in an alternate time period and must know his persona inside and out. He must also have the ability to put visitors at ease and draw them into that world. Some visitors do not want to go along with the pretense. The interpreter must be convincing and provide enough focus to mitigate the ever-present twenty-first-century distractions. He must know whether or not to acknowledge a ringing cell phone or an airplane overhead and must be skillful in a specific accent, if required. When the fourth wall does disappear, it can be a fascinating teaching moment. In Williamsburg, the opportunity for a one-on-one encounter with a person playing an enslaved eighteenth-century resident or even a teenaged member of the gentry class makes for an active experience. Often character interpreters will draw visitors into the tasks they are involved in . . . from dancing or playing games to work activities.

Unfortunately or fortunately, I can't decide which, my internship did not afford the opportunity to dress in colonial attire. At one point the staff talked of putting together a lawn bowling team to demonstrate the eighteenth-century game. I was ready to don the knee breeches and tri-corner hat and bowl my heart out, but it was not to be. In years since my summer in Williamsburg, my former colleagues have talked of reenacting cricket games, pig roasts, horse races, and other fun activities.

Over recent decades, millions of people from around the world have visited Colonial Williamsburg. People from all walks of life stroll the main street, Duke of Gloucester, to "experience" history. They watch tradesmen plying eighteenth-century trades: assembling barrels, weaving wigs, cutting shoe leather, and carving musical instruments. They tour stately homes, gardens, and the regal Governor's Palace. They participate in dramatized courthouse trials, debates at the Capitol building, and militia drills on the green. They pose for countless photos with head and arms clamped in the pillory or feet in the stocks. Some visitors embrace this form of experiential learning, while others view it as ridiculous playacting, an eighteenth-century renaissance fair.

When John D. Rockefeller Jr. decided to fund the multimillion-dollar restoration project, he wanted to promote Williamsburg's role as the breeding ground for American patriots. He claimed the restoration taught "patriotism, high purpose, and unselfish devotion of our forefathers to the common good." As the largest colony in America, Virginia held strong ties to England. The state church was the Anglican Church, and the British governor, representing the Crown, presided in a "palace" in Williamsburg. While the gentry class educated their sons in England, these colonial leaders began to develop a growing sense of freedom. In this swirling crucible where independence was debated and finally declared in 1775, the lessons still apply today. The founders of Colonial Williamsburg recognized the value of teaching this story of new freedom to their young visitors. But history is not just one story, it is many.

Deciding What Stories To Tell

Staff at every history museum must make decisions about what content they will teach and how they will teach it. Of the thousands of stories to be told of Williamsburg, which rise to the top as most worthy, profitable, and educational? Rockefeller's generosity preserved eighty-eight original buildings and allowed for the reconstruction of many others—but buildings have a limited capacity to speak for themselves. Regardless of which stories are shared by the Colonial Williamsburg interpreters, the story of freedom will always be told. Williamsburg cannot stray from its patriotic core. But over time the interpretation changed. From a Disneyfied past has emerged a dirty past, one that makes bold attempts at authenticity. Today Williamsburg does a commendable job of confronting visitors with the complexity of our history.

In the 1930s Williamsburg's "storytellers" focused on reproducing a preindustrial culture. They highlighted graceful architecture and a beautiful city with rural craftsmen and genteel dwellings. As America moved into war in the 1940s, the U.S. government made Williamsburg an intentional stop for many GIs traveling through Virginia. The soldiers learned about patriots such as Patrick Henry, George Washington, and Thomas Jefferson who stood their ground for freedom and whose debate of liberty contributed to the founding of the United States. In the following decades of the Cold War, the ideals of democracy and the principles of liberty grew even more important. Williamsburg became a prime family destination for parents who wanted to instill these values in their children.

However, as the unrest of the 1960s spread around the country, a new focus of history began to gain attention and acceptance. Whereas past political history featured the great men who molded the fabric of a country, this new history, termed social history, focused on the everyday lives of ordinary people. Gradually, historians began to pay attention to African American history and women's history and the history of the underclasses. This shift profoundly affected the stories told at Williamsburg.

By the early 1980s Colonial Williamsburg had established a department that would research and present programs about African Americans in the colonial town. In the eighteenth century free and enslaved blacks made up more than half of the town's eighteen hundred inhabitants. This shift in interpretive focus was not the result of new historical evidence, but a recognition that this story should be told.

The majority of blacks in colonial Virginia were enslaved. In many ways Williamsburg's move to tell this story was a risky action fraught with challenges and considered radical by some. It raised many questions: How would the inclusion of this uncomfortable story affect the mostly white visitors? Would the story attract more African American visitors? Would they want to hear about slavery? Slavery is an uncomfortable topic for people in general, but especially people on vacation who choose to spend their leisure time at Williamsburg. Given Williamsburg's presentation method of historical reenactment, would African American staff be willing to portray an enslaved people day after day? How accurate can one be when talking about slavery?

Historian Freeman Tilden wrote a seminal book for the National Park Service in 1957 that often serves as a reference for history museum staffs. The book describes guiding principles related to presenting history to the public. One of the principles states that the chief aim of presenting history should not be instruction but provocation. Provoking thought means piquing one's interest. Williamsburg has embraced this concept.

The Interpreters Training Manual at the time of my internship stated, "Visitors to Colonial Williamsburg should be challenged and provoked by their visit. Their experience with eighteenth-century Williamsburg should jar them out of their present-mindedness and compel them to reconsider their understanding of the past."

No topic has quite the potential to provoke thought like American slavery.

With its decision to tackle the topic of slavery head on, Williamsburg accepted a major challenge. Its directors made great strides over several decades in their efforts to educate visitors about the complexities of slavery. Through innovative programs and characters, they attempted to provide visitors a glimpse into life as an enslaved person in America. Actors portray slaves confronted by a patrol looking for escaped slaves or slaves doing daily work in the slave quarters. In the 1770s, when white Americans were talking about freedom for themselves and trying to define their rights, African American slaves couldn't fail to notice the irony.

A Risky Experiment

Williamsburg's most famous program made headlines around the world. On a fall day in 1994 staff reenacted an estate auction in which four slaves were sold to the highest bidder. This controversial event, part of normal life in eighteenth-century Virginia, was designed to provoke thought about a brutal aspect of American slavery. While I didn't witness the auction reenactment, I talked with colleagues afterward and got the inside perspective. The program was an experimental new program and was in testing stage. Staff had expected a small crowd of visitors because they had not marketed it. Carefully outlined but not scripted, the event was based on historical precedent, part of a reenactment of Public Times, a public event held during the meeting of the colony's General Court. The auction featured three sales, chosen specifically to reflect some of the variables that affected a slave's price: age, skill set, and pregnancy.

Somehow word about the reenactment leaked to the press and suddenly became national news. Voices of disapproval grew louder by the day. People protested to state chapters of the NAACP, afraid that the event would trivialize slavery. Others felt that the subject should stay in the past and not be rehashed. On the scheduled day, in the minutes before the auction was set to begin, a crowd was building outside, while inside Colonial Williamsburg executives were split on whether or not to hold the program. The "cast" had discussed contingencies: what to do if things got out of hand, belligerent crowd members, as well as boundaries—limits on the words they would and would not use. They decided that the N-word was off limits. While historically accurate, it would have been more divisive than productive.

As the executives huddled and the cast prayed for calm, a small group of protesters shouted at the top of their lungs that the event should not take place. Members of the large crowd then began booing the protesters. When a staff member finally emerged to announce that the show would go on, the crowd erupted with cheers, though a few protesters continued to shout. An extreme hush fell over the crowd as the staff member explained why they were presenting the program—to educate people about a historical topic.

Then the bidding got underway. Positioned in the first couple of rows, staff members portraying bidders interacted with the visitors. They commented on worthiness, condition, looks . . . the rapt crowd was respectful and willing to engage, but found it awkward to discuss people as commodities. The program went extremely well. The circumstances of the final sale threatened to split up a family. The crowd members were visibly moved by the portent, some demanding that one of the bidders up his bid to keep the family together. A wave of disappointment swept the crowd when he refused, with a curt dismissal of the slave as an investment.

In the end the protesters that attended the program were apparently satisfied with Williamsburg's faithfulness to historical fact and sensitivity to the topic. They said they understood why Williamsburg presented the auction and why it was a valuable exercise. Ultimately decency could not allow the event to show in vivid detail the depth of inhumanity at a slave auction, but Williamsburg's willingness to stand firm and attempt to spark discussion about America's past can only be admired. My colleagues described an impressive and lengthy applause at the end and people lingering long afterward to hear historians provide context and discuss the experience. One of my colleagues recounted her pride at the decision to go forward with the program. While no formal evaluation was completed, it was obvious that the crowd was deeply moved that day.

A Revolutionary Program

From my cubicle on the second floor of the white-frame James Anderson House, a structure on Duke of Gloucester Street built around 1770, I could look out at the reconstructed building that housed Anderson's blacksmith shop. I heard the clang of the anvil every day as tradesmen operated the forges, showing visitors how blacksmiths crafted a variety of metalwork, from intricate scrollwork patterns on elaborate gates to mundane horseshoes and nails.

My intern project provided me with a fascinating look at the encounters between costumed interpreters and visitors. Charged with designing and implementing a survey to quantify these encounters, I collected data detailing the amount and kinds of interaction. I timed how long visitors stayed at certain sites and recorded the ways in which interpreters offered visitors opportunities to join in an activity such as learning a dance step or the proper way to curtsy. The data showed a good amount of interaction and allowed staff to set a baseline for future evaluation.

In the years since, Williamsburg has moved toward increased interaction between interpreters and visitors. In 2006 the site instituted the Revolutionary City program, an experiment in street theater where crowds meet at a specific place and character interpreters begin telling a story that intersects with characters in other locations throughout the town. In this carefully choreographed production, the crowd follows the story from one place to the next and hears multiple perspectives.

One Revolutionary City program I witnessed portrayed the events leading up to Virginia's resolution to declare independence. It began with the Royal Governor, Lord Dunmore, arriving by carriage at the Capitol. He was unhappy with the House of Burgesses for protesting the closing of Boston Harbor by the British government, so he disbanded the government. In the next scene, almost a year had passed, and the crowd learned that Dunmore had ordered the removal of gunpowder from the Public Magazine. Some patriots threatened retaliation, but a notable citizen stepped in and arranged a truce. Then a messenger galloped in on horseback, bringing the stunning news from the north of the battles of Lexington and Concord. Suddenly Virginians had to decide whether to support their northern neighbors or stay loyal to the Crown.

We next listened in on an uncomfortable confrontation between a mother and her teenage daughter. In a family ripped apart by opposing loyalties, the father remained loyal to the Crown while the son had chosen patriotism. The daughter, tired of the looks and whispers she received around town, lashed out at her mother. What teenage visitor couldn't relate? In rapid succession viewers were swept up in scenes of life in 1775, encouraged to join a riotous crowd and allowed to overhear a private conversation.

A loyalist caught in an angry patriotic crowd barely avoided the colonial punishment of tar and feathers. After Dunmore proclaimed freedom for slaves who joined the King's cause, a discussion ensued between Williamsburg's slaves to consider this enticing opportunity. What were the benefits and dangers of this unlikely offer? In another scene, a carpenter who had fallen on hard times argued with his wife about enlisting in the army. The heart-wrenching conversation conveyed the wife's concerns about the family during his absence.

Finally, the crowd moved to the south lawn of the Capitol building, where Virginia's representatives to the Continental Congress voted on resolutions to declare Virginia's independence. Would they pass? The crowd waited in anticipation. Although they knew the outcome from their history books, the drama of the moment had captured their imagination. A man emerged from the Capitol to announce that the Congress had done it! They had voted to cut ties with Britain. There was no turning back. The crowd roared its approval. As a cannon boomed and fifes trilled, the Union Jack was lowered from its place above the Capitol and a flag representing the thirteen colonies was raised. The audience could not help but be drawn into the emotion of the moment.

The carefully crafted script illustrated multiple perspectives. In times past only the leading patriots' views would have been featured. Today's programs reveal the myriad decisions everyday people were forced to make: slaves agonizing over whether or not to run to the British side, teenagers trying to figure out their personal loyalties, and a husband and wife questioning a major decision that will impact the family's well-being. These are scenarios clearly designed to resonate with visitors from all age groups, walks of life, and racial backgrounds. They challenge visitors to ponder what they might do if placed in any one of these situations. We are two hundred years removed from the decisions presented in the scenarios, yet they are not so very distant. As William Faulkner wrote, "The past is never dead. It's not even past."

If experience is defined as a "direct participation in events," then Williamsburg's visitors do experience history. Whether it's in the personal one-on-one encounters with Thomas Jefferson or among the highly charged crowds cheering a declaration of independence, visitors receive a glimpse into lives not so distant from their own. Humanity's aspirations, joys, and depravities transcend time and place. Maybe, as critics continue to charge, Williamsburg is too clean and pristine to be historically accurate—little manure on the streets, no body odor or human waste smells lingering in the wind, no chaos of an inhabited city with animals loose in the streets. Maybe it is unable to adequately explore the reality of human slavery. Yet despite these critiques, the restored city offers the rare opportunity to jump in feet first and try to understand life more than two hundred years ago, to visit the foreign country that is the past and to see that human nature was not so different then.

My Williamsburg internship, more observation than anything else, proved a vital foundation block for my entire history career. It offered an opportunity to watch visitor interactions day after day and to ponder larger questions about history and learning. And it confirmed my interest in the educational function of a history organization. No quiet archives or collections storage rooms for me—I wanted to help history come alive for others.

3
CHALLENGING HISTORY

I, John Brown, am now quite certain that
the crimes of this guilty land will never
be purged away but with Blood.

—*John Brown, 1859*

Not every person employed in a history profession gets to work in
a grand or fascinating historic building. Though I've rarely had a
window in my offices, I have been fortunate to go to work every day
in beautiful buildings with interesting histories. In Williamsburg
I worked from a restored eighteenth-century house on the Duke
of Gloucester Street. Next, my first paid history position placed
me in one of the grandest buildings in Washington DC, one with
a history that rivals that of the most well-known buildings in our
nation's capital.

A Building's Story

The National Portrait Gallery occupies the third oldest public building in the city and sits north of the National Mall on Eighth and F

Streets. The magnificent Greek Revival structure was built to house the United States Patent Office. Begun in 1836, construction of all four wings was not completed until 1868, when it became the largest office building in the United States, covering several city blocks. As a portrait gallery it literally holds thousands of faces from the past. But the building itself has seen its share of national history and has many stories to tell. It remains one of my favorite buildings in Washington.

The first wing opened in 1840, and the public quickly dubbed the enormous vaulted room on the third floor the National Gallery. Some claimed it was the largest exhibition hall in America and for a short time, before the Smithsonian existed, it was known as a "museum of curiosities"; almost a hundred thousand visitors per year came to wonder at its eclectic displays: the Declaration of Independence; relics owned by George Washington, including his Continental army tent; a piece of Plymouth Rock; portraits of Indian chiefs commissioned by the War Department; specimens from expeditions to the Pacific; and items brought back from Commodore Perry's visit to Japan.

The building served as a hospital for about a year and a half during the Civil War. Almost three thousand beds accommodating wounded soldiers lined its corridors. President and Mrs. Lincoln visited the troops, as did the poet Walt Whitman, who described the scene: "[T]hat noblest of Washington buildings was crowded close with rows of sick, badly wounded and dying soldiers. . . . I went there many times." He brought small gifts, read to the soldiers, played games with and wrote letters for them. Another famous American, Clara Barton, came to Washington from Massachusetts in 1854 and was hired by the patent commissioner as his confidential clerk. Her association with the building continued during the war, when she tended the wounded there. She went on to promote life-saving medical care on the battlefields, later founding the American Red Cross.

President Lincoln held his second inaugural ball in the large room on the third floor. What an event it must have been. Many guests most likely did not remember the dancing or the presence of President and Mrs. Lincoln. The memorable moment took place at midnight, when supper was announced. A 250-foot-long buffet table set up among model cases featured, among other delicacies, oyster and terrapin stews; beef à l'anglais; smoked tongue en gelée; ornamental pyramids of nougat, orange, coconut, and caramel with fancy cream candy; calf's foot and wine jellies; ice creams; and fruit ices. Several large confectionary depictions decorated the table, a huge U.S. Capitol serving as the centerpiece. With an estimated four thousand guests in attendance, the buffet table was designed to accommodate three hundred at a time. The call to supper resulted in a mad rush and absolute chaos ensued. The following day the *New York Times* described the moment: "In less than an hour the table was a wreck . . . positively frightful to behold." The *Washington Evening Star* reported, "The floor of the supper room was soon sticky, pasty and oily with wasted confections, mashed cake, and debris of fowl and meat."

In 1877 more than two hundred thousand small patent models representing the innovation of a nation were on display, crammed into nine-foot-high cases that stretched down corridors for almost a quarter of a mile. Whitman wrote that "two of the immense apartments are fill'd with high and ponderous glass cases, crowded with models in miniature of every kind of . . . invention, it ever enter'd into the mind of man to conceive." Seventh Street, on the eastern side of the building, became a principal retail district in the city, and the surrounding neighborhood soon filled with patent attorneys, model makers, and draftsmen. The nineteenth-century public enjoyed viewing the models, but by 1908 their fascination had waned and most of the models were moved into storage. In 1926 the Patent Office disposed of its models, the Smithsonian selecting six thousand of them for its growing national collections.

By the mid-1900s, the structure was in bad shape. The Patent Office had moved out and the current tenant, the Civil Service

Commission, was eager for a new building. Congress introduced legislation to demolish the building and replace it with a parking garage. Fortunately, a three-year opposition effort and a last-minute order from President Eisenhower saved the piece of history from the wrecking ball, and in 1958 Congress transferred the dilapidated building to the Smithsonian Institution. Ten years later this early example of historic preservation was transformed into two gems in the Smithsonian crown—the National Portrait Gallery and the National Museum of American Art (now the Smithsonian American Art Museum).

My First Paid History Job

My association with this beautiful building began on a cold early spring day in 1992. A graduate student, I was fuzzy about where my degree in history would lead me and desperately sought some kind of practical experience. At the recommendation of a friend, I scheduled an informational interview with the Curator of Education at the National Portrait Gallery. After an hour with this gregarious, energetic man, my eyes were opened to the field of museum education, and I had secured a solid lead for a job and discovered a place that continues to enthrall me to this day.

With its unique blend of art and biography, the Portrait Gallery proved an excellent training ground for a young historian. The following fall, after my summer in Williamsburg, I began work as a lowly education aide. Our team of eight aides was a mixed group with eclectic backgrounds: people trained in art history, art, theater, education, and history, along with a former Postal Service employee. We gave tours of the collection and presented educational programs to secondary school students in classrooms around the Washington DC area and to senior adult groups in retirement facilities. We bonded while getting lost on the tangle of DC streets and gained valuable insight into the challenges teachers face. The trained musicians in the group presented programs featuring the music of well-known American composers such as Richard Rogers and Oscar Hammerstein, Cole Porter and Ira and George Gershwin. We had various motives—for some it was an opportunity to get paid to perform, for others it was a first opportunity to get paid as a historian. We stood on the brink of nascent careers, some in the world of museums. My three years at the Portrait Gallery laid an exceptional groundwork for a career in museum education and history. The programs I presented covered tough topics like racial inequality and stretched me in numerous ways. I learned to engage all ages with America's challenging history.

Looking Behind the Faces

Famous and infamous faces from American history line the walls of the Portrait Gallery. For me, a walk through its corridors is like a walk through a county fair where I run into old acquaintances at every turn. The faces look familiar and I know I've met these people before. They come straight from the pages of my American history textbooks—only these are the originals.

I see not only the famous—presidents, athletes, and celebrities—but also the infamous—corrupt politicians, criminals, and the unfamous, those who failed to make the textbooks. People like Belva Ann Lockwood, the first female lawyer to argue a case before the Supreme Court and first woman to run for president. Lockwood's name appeared on every state ballot in 1884—years before women's suffrage took effect—and she received four thousand votes. Or Willie "the Lion" Smith. In the 1920s this New York jazz pianist directly influenced the music of Duke Ellington. Or Lillian Wald, one of America's greatest social workers. I always meet someone new.

The portraits come in all shapes, sizes, and styles. The variety of media alone makes a walk down the halls simply fascinating. You might see a carved Rosa Parks or a sculpted Rachel Carson, or even a portrait made from hand-painted Lite-Brite pegs. While the "sitters"—portrait subjects—get the most attention, sometimes elaborate gilt frames compete for the eye.

Madman or Martyr

A singularly compelling portrait in the collection depicts an older white man with penetrating blue eyes and a wild head of gray hair. His sharp nose sits atop a flowing white mustache and beard. A white shirt collar is visible around his neck, his body wrapped in a gray wool blanket. The intensity of his gaze reflects a jumble of emotions, including sadness and resignation. Many Americans would not recognize either his image or his name. Historians have debated his role in America's past—perhaps he is the ultimate American provocateur. His actions in Kansas and later in Harpers Ferry, Virginia, made newspaper headlines around the country. Some historians give him credit for lighting the final spark that brought about the conflagration of the Civil War. Labeled a villain, terrorist, madman, martyr, and saint, John Brown remains a controversial figure in history.

During my years giving tours at the gallery, I stopped to show Brown's portrait to many students. The picture became one of my favorites due to its passion and starkness. The viewer cannot fail to wonder who this person was and what cause drove his soul. Even teenagers, undoubtedly one of the most challenging audiences, were drawn to the painting. Brown's story represents the power of biography to engage people with the past. His colorful life ended in a dark thundercloud of tension on the gallows, and his legacy represents the power of one person to make a difference in the world.

Brown's life story reached its climax at Harpers Ferry (now in West Virginia), just slightly over an hour's drive from Washington. The tiny town tumbles down a steep hillside at the confluence of two of America's great rivers: the Shenandoah and the Potomac. Three states meet here in this peaceful place that today is home to Harpers Ferry National Historic Park. Although it boasts a long and fascinating history, the town is best known for one brief event in the nation's past: John Brown's raid on its federal arsenal.

In 1798 Congress selected Harpers Ferry as the site for one of only two federal arsenals and armories. Due to its strategic location, it quickly became an important transportation hub. In the spring of 1803 Meriwether Lewis visited the Harpers Ferry armory to obtain guns for his expedition west. By 1859 a large booming industrial complex stood on the Potomac River at the town's edge.

John Brown, a militant abolitionist, hatched a daring plan to raid the federal arsenal in order to arm nearby slaves and begin a slave revolt he anticipated would spread throughout the slave states. The Captain, as Brown was known to his men, secretly raised money to put together an "army" of twenty-one men who would carry out the attack. Late on the evening of October 16, 1859, he and his men silently crossed the railroad bridge from Maryland, moved into town, and quickly captured the armory. The citizens of Harpers Ferry raised the alarm of insurrection and eventually a group of marines from Washington under the command of Col. Robert E. Lee trapped Brown in the engine house. His war ended just thirty-six hours after it had begun and not a single slave had joined his effort. His subsequent trial, conviction, and hanging vilified him in the South while many in the North revered him as a martyr.

A Powerful Program

John Brown's raid provided the basis for one of the Portrait Gallery's most popular school programs. The "Trial of John Brown," based loosely on his actual trial, put students in the jury box.

The jury filed in, not silent as most juries, but noisy and eager. They were not a diverse group—all were young and all African American.

"Hear ye, hear ye, the county court of Jefferson County, Virginia, Judge Walter Wright presiding, is now in session. All rise for the judge."

The judge banged his gavel.

"The court will now come to order. The case before us is that of the State of Virginia versus John Brown. Ladies and gentlemen of the jury, John Brown is charged by the State of Virginia with murder, conspiracy to incite slaves to rebellion, and treason against the state of Virginia."

The trial went on for a long time and three witnesses described the character of John Brown. They testified to their relationships with Brown and recounted the events of October 16 and 17, 1859. An abolitionist Boston banker spoke of Brown's request for funding the attack. A Maryland farmer who lived near Brown's rented farm described events leading up to the raid and provided details of the raid. And an escaped slave living in Canada spoke firsthand of the cruelties of slavery.

The judge called for closing statements: "Ladies and gentlemen of the jury . . . you have been called here today to answer a simple question: Did John Brown break the law? That's it. Not 'Is slavery morally wrong?' Slavery, I'll remind you, is the accepted law in the state of Virginia. Now, if you have troubles with that law, there are methods to change that law. Peaceful, legal methods. . . . Did John Brown break the law? Yes! The state's law, the federal law, and God's law. You must find him guilty. He has slaughtered decent human beings and would slaughter more—children, women, black or white. In death he does not discriminate. And for that, John Brown must pay with his life." With that the prosecutor rested his case and sat down, slowly, for dramatic effect.

The defense attorney rose: "My colleague would have you condemn John Brown for rising up to strike down what he felt was an intolerable situation. If you condemn John Brown for following his conscience, you then must condemn Moses. Was Moses wrong to free his people? If you condemn John Brown, you condemn the Negro race in this country to further degradation. If you hang John Brown, you hang the rights of every black man and woman in America. You have an opportunity right here, right now, to say 'This is wrong!' Seize that opportunity!"

With one final firm glance at the jury, he turned and went back to his seat.

The judge looked at the jury. "What say you?"

The vote was unanimous. "Not guilty."

As it turned out, the jury was fickle. In this scripted program the evidence remained the same and both the prosecuting and defense attorneys eloquently pleaded their case, but the verdict changed with each student jury, often tied to the racial mix of the students. No matter how ardent the prosecuting attorney's argument that Virginia law clearly required a guilty vote, time and time again classes refused to convict Brown.

According to 1859 Virginia law, Brown was guilty of the three charges against him. With great passion, students argued his humanitarian cause, a springboard to discussion of how one goes about reacting to a law with which he or she may not agree. We discussed the various ways one can protest a law. Is it ever permissible to take the law into one's own hands? The program provided many connections to the present and helped students see the relevance of history. A National Park Service historian once said, "Americans do not deliberate about John Brown—they *feel* him. He is still alive today in the American soul. He represents something for each of us, but none of us is in agreement about what he means."

The "Trial of John Brown" still ranks as one of the most effective and engaging school programs that I have ever encountered because it presented evidence and asked for a response. Like most mock trials, it afforded students the opportunity to understand a bit about our laws and the judicial system. It also challenged students to think about the democratic ways to influence law. It introduced students to this divisive figure and pivotal event in American history. And it made history fun.

Visiting Harpers Ferry

I first visited Harpers Ferry during my years at the Portrait Gallery and continue to return to walk the cobblestoned streets and soak in its history. I enjoy strolling across the railroad bridge spanning the Potomac River and climbing the steep trail to Maryland Heights for a sweeping view of the town and confluence. I can imagine the clanging and shouts coming from the busy armory complex. But the focal point of any visit is John Brown's fort, as the engine house became known. As the place where his vision came to a sudden end, the small redbrick building is a survivor and its story demonstrates the dedication of many followers who wished to preserve the memory of John Brown.

In the decades after the raid, the fort became a symbol of abolition and the site a respected destination for African American tourists. An enterprising organization later known as the John Brown Fort Company purchased the structure and paid to move it to the 1893 Columbian Exposition in Chicago. Several years later a newspaper reporter from Washington convinced a local farmer near Harpers Ferry to provide land on his farm where the fort could be reconstructed. In its new location the fort continued to attract the attention of people desiring to pay homage to John Brown.

As the struggle for racial equality became more organized and gained strength, two prominent groups visited the fort. The National League of Colored Women held its first national convention in 1896, and attendees traveled to the farm to view the fort. Then in 1906, W. E. B. Du Bois led the second meeting of the Niagara Movement, often thought to be the precursor to the NAACP. The meeting took place in Harpers Ferry and included a brief trip to the holy ground of John Brown's fort.

Shortly after this momentous event, trustees of Storer College, a technical school for freed slaves located in Harpers Ferry, bought the fort, moved it to their campus, and turned it into a museum. Due to the fort's multiple relocations, many pieces were lost to souvenir hunters and the structure badly needed a major renovation. The establishment of Harpers Ferry National Historical Park in the following years saw several attempts by the National Park Service to acquire the fort and return it to its original location at the lower end of town. Finally the Park Service purchased the fort and in 1968 successfully moved the structure to its present site.

Today the lower section of Harpers Ferry, restored to its mid-nineteenth-century appearance, is part of Harpers Ferry National Historical Park, forever preserved for the American people. Exhibitions in various buildings tell stories of the town's past, including John Brown's raid, occupation during the Civil War, major floods, the armory's bosses and workers, Storer College, and the Niagara Movement. The engine house sits close to its original location on that chaotic fall night, silently reminding visitors of the cost of protest.

African American History Lessons

My time at the National Portrait Gallery taught me many things about history, about museums, and about people. Most important, it spurred me to think about different perspectives of history. I saw history through the eyes of classrooms that were largely African American. I learned about the richness of the Harlem Renaissance and the complexities of the drive for racial equality. I guided students in discussions about various historical views on women's suffrage.

One of the strengths of the educational programs at the gallery was their focus on role play. A variety of programs challenged students to play the roles of people from the past. Whether as a resident of colonial Connecticut or a settler headed west on the Oregon Trail, the students had the opportunity to take on a specific character designed to demonstrate differing perspectives and to promote discussion. In other words, when we successfully convinced teens to suspend disbelief, play along, and forget about what their peers might think of them, it worked well.

Most educators know that younger children, lacking inhibitions, are willing to role play. The older the students, the harder it is to convince them to participate. Teenagers are hypersensitive to any possible risk of embarrassment and fear they will say something stupid. However, I found that a provocative statement often did the trick. Statements such as "Women don't have the mental capacity to vote" or "The answer is to move back to Africa" were sure to spark a lively discussion.

One of my favorite school programs at the Portrait Gallery was called "I, Too, Am America," inspired by the poem by Langston Hughes. In this role-playing exercise set in Harlem's 191st Street Baptist Church, three staff members played recruiters representing 1920s views on how to improve life for America's blacks. The class represented a diverse group of people gathered to discuss the challenges of improving the condition of the black race in America. The program began with a background slide lecture that helped students visualize the stark conditions of the time, highlighting supposed "separate but equal" conditions, the cruelty to black soldiers recently returned from World War I, and the harsh reality of lynchings. After setting the scene, each "recruiter" would briefly discuss his or her views.

One staff member espoused Booker T. Washington's philosophy. The founder of the Tuskegee Institute and former slave believed in the dignity of labor and self-help. He said, "There is as much dignity in tilling a field as there is in writing a poem." He believed economic power would lead to political equality. "No race that has anything to contribute to the market of the world is long ostracized." Industrial education would meet practical needs and with patience in matters of racial injustice, change would eventually come. He professed that gradually, through working, lives would improve.

Another staff member represented W. E. B. Du Bois's "talented tenth" philosophy, an emphasis on the importance of education and the need for the top tenth of black society to take leading roles in the drive to improve relations. A leader of the Niagara Movement and founder of the NAACP, Du Bois wanted immediate change and believed that it could not come until blacks were educated.

A final staff member advocated for Marcus Garvey and his famous Back to Africa movement. Garvey established the Universal Negro Improvement Association to unite the black people of the world by founding a nation in Africa "where race will be given the fullest opportunity to develop itself, such as may not be expected in countries where we form but a minority in a majority government of other races." Garvey was on a mission to encourage American blacks to immigrate to Africa. He also believed strongly in supporting black businesses by "buying black," so that blacks in America could become as independent as possible. He believed in racial segregation as a means to preserve the black race.

Each student was given a paper detailing the background of a person attending the event. As the discussion progressed, the carefully researched profiles enabled students to actively contribute most of the commonly held views regarding ways to improve conditions. Roles were based on real people from all walks of life: Bert Williams, a popular entertainer in Harlem clubs that catered to whites; Lula Mae Griffin, a young hat check girl in Chicago; Hattie Clay, a domestic in New York. Our mission was to motivate students to think critically about the advantages and disadvantages of each theory and the gray areas that existed for African Americans.

At the end of the class period, the students voted on which of the three viewpoints they supported. A class that concluded with passionate shouts from students trying to convince their classmates to change their minds was music to our ears. Discussion often grew quite lively and the louder it became, the more successful our program seemed. The program taught students that history is full of differing perspectives. If nothing else, I hope they learned that there is an underlying complexity to history and that it's worth pursuing a deeper understanding of why people acted the way they did. This program and others like it taught me that the smallest attempts to put myself in someone else's shoes leads a bit closer to understanding.

Reopening the National Portrait Gallery

When I left my job at the Portrait Gallery in 1995, the building was in need of repair. It sat in a desolate neighborhood, across the street from the empty government building that once housed the city's original General Post Office. New restaurants would open and then soon close their doors due to lack of business. The gem of a building sat in a neglected part of town. All of this changed within eleven years.

Today, the neighborhood, Penn Quarter, has become one of the hottest spots in town. Thousands of hockey and basketball fans cheer for the city's teams in an arena across the street. A boutique hotel occupies the old post office building. Dozens of restaurants line the streets. And, in 2006, after closing for six years of renovation, the Old Patent Office building opened once again, a gleaming space transformed. The National Portrait Gallery and American Art Museum still share the building, but a new layout blends collections into a stunning display of American history. The building sparkles with shiny tiles and its natural light–infused rooms are filled with colorful art. The landscaped courtyard with its stately elm trees, Calder sculptures, and historic cast-iron fountains is gone, paved and covered over with a famous glass canopy by the renowned British architect Norman Foster. The tulip beds will not bloom again, but despite changes, the building retains its power to speak through time.

The Lincoln gallery on the third floor, site of Lincoln's second inaugural ball, looks very different than it did 150 years ago. The large expansive room houses the American Art Museum's modern art pieces. Almost 600 feet of brightly colored neon lights form a large vertical map of the United States featuring 336 televisions of different sizes—an art installation by Nam June Paik. Titled the *Electronic Superhighway: Continental U.S.*, the piece offers a statement about individual state identity in the information age.

Looking closely at one of the room's interior window frames, a visitor will find "C.H.F." and the date August 8, 1864, faintly scratched into the woodwork. Is it a bit of Civil War–era graffiti left by a Union soldier? Was he alone, or with a group of friends? Or more likely, it was a Patent Office employee wanting to leave his mark. Young, old, far from home? So many questions. We'll never know. But in a small way one person's simple act of destruction helps bridge the distances of time, and perhaps his spirit lingers when the lights go out at night. Perhaps his is one of the faces staring out from one of the Civil War–era daguerreotypes on display.

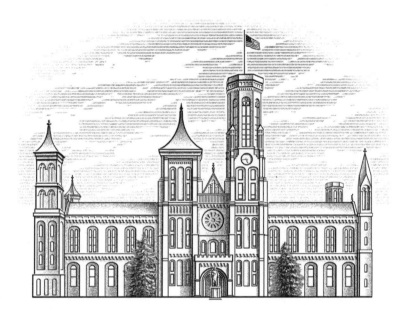

4
THE
EVEREST
OF MUSEUMS

I bequeath the whole of my property . . . to the United States of America, to found at Washington, under the name of the Smithsonian Institution, an Establishment for the increase and diffusion of knowledge among men.

—*James Smithson's will*

Stand with me on the rooftop patio of the National Museum of American History. To our west, the Washington Monument rises into the sky, beckoning us to reach out a hand and touch it. Turn around, and the spotty green of the National Mall sweeps our eyes to the Capitol Building situated majestically beyond the reflecting pool. Lining both sides of the Mall, a great architectural mix of famous buildings form the core of the Smithsonian museum family.

In 1996 I stood here on the roof to watch fireworks marking the 150th anniversary of the Smithsonian Institution. The yearlong celebration events included a national tour of Smithsonian treasures, special exhibitions at the various museums, and a weekend festival in August culminating with a concert and fireworks.

In addition to a fireworks display over the grounds of the Washington Monument, the anniversary show featured a second series of fireworks launched from behind the Castle, the Smithsonian's main administrative building, which sits on the south side of the National Mall. Spectacular bursts of colored light silhouetted the multiturreted red sandstone building. The sight remains etched in my memory—the red, white, and blue sprays of sparks appeared to come right out of the building itself, giving the illusion of a building on fire. This was a rare opportunity for staff members to enjoy the view. As I watched the astounding dual display with my colleagues, I counted my blessings and silently celebrated my new permanent position at the Smithsonian.

Mr. Smithson's Gift

In the mountain ranges of the museum world, the Smithsonian is Mt. Everest. As America's premier cultural institution and the world's largest museum complex, the Smithsonian attracts museum people like the Hollywood glow lures actors. The gleaming buildings along the National Mall call out a siren song, but landing a Smithsonian job can be next to impossible: Competition is fierce. Positions are rare because relatively few employees leave. Job satisfaction is high.

The Smithsonian brand holds great recognition among all market groups and is considered highly trustworthy. More than 90 percent of Americans recognize the Smithsonian name. Since its founding in 1846, the institution has grown and morphed into a hugely complex national organization. It is not one monumental building in Washington, as some visitors believe when they arrive, but nineteen museums, the National Zoo, and nine scientific research centers with units in seven states, as well as in Panama and Belize.

Many Americans aren't aware that the Smithsonian exists because of the generous and somewhat odd gift of a British scientist, James Smithson, who never set foot on American shores. Smithson's will, written in 1826, named his nephew as beneficiary. A short clause at the end stipulated that, should the nephew die without heirs, the estate should go "to the United States of America, to found at Washington, under the name of the Smithsonian Institution, an Establishment for the increase and diffusion of knowledge among men." Smithson passed away in 1829 and six years later, his nephew died without children. The Smithson money ended up in the care of the executors. As author Nina Burleigh describes it, "It was their duty to notify the American president of a peculiar sentence at the very bottom of Smithson's will, a sentence that would profoundly affect American cultural life for centuries." After three years of lawsuits and legal proceedings, U.S. Emissary Richard Rush disembarked from the ship *Mediator* in New York with one hundred and five sacks of gold sovereigns packed into boxes—half a million dollars or the rough equivalent of fifty million dollars today.

Former president John Quincy Adams, then a congressman and chair of the House committee that would debate the outcome of the gift, had mixed feelings. He immediately identified the hand of Providence in the act, and called it "an event . . . compassing great results by incomprehensible means." Yet while impressed with the benevolence of Smithson, a "stranger to this country," he wisely did not have a lot of confidence in his colleagues in Congress. Some were already questioning the motive of the gift, suspicious of an Englishman. Privately he wondered what would become of the money: "Whether this bequest will ever come to anything is much doubted by almost everyone," he wrote in 1836. "I proceed with a heavy heart from a presentiment that this noble and most munificent donation will be filtered to nothing and wasted upon hungry and worthless political jackals." Nevertheless, he told his fellow legislators that "to furnish the means of acquiring knowledge is . . . the greatest benefit that can be conferred upon mankind."

Arguments over what to do with the gift lasted eleven years, the subject of over four hundred discussions in the Senate and fifty-seven in the House. The many ideas to satisfy the terms of the bequest included a national school, an agricultural college with a working farm, a great national library, and a scientific institution. Finally the proponents of science won out and seventeen years after Smithson's death, Congress passed an act, signed by President James Polk on August 10, 1846, establishing the Institution. The act provided for a building housing a museum, an art gallery, a chemical laboratory, and a library. It further directed that all art and natural history objects then belonging to the federal government in Washington should be given to the Institution. The city of Washington became the great beneficiary. In the mid-nineteenth century, the logical place to locate such an institution of science and learning would have been New York, Philadelphia, or Boston. The fact that Smithson had specified Washington suddenly meant the city would finally have a small foundation of culture that would flourish and grow in the years ahead.

Today visitors to Washington can tour the Smithsonian's original building, the Castle, sitting on the National Mall between the Capitol and the Washington Monument. The Castle was designed by noted architect James Renwick, who later built St. Patrick's Cathedral in midtown Manhattan, and construction was completed in 1855. Though only in his twenties at the time, Renwick won the design competition and his new building was an early example of Medieval Revival. Its eight distinct towers rise from an asymmetrical layout. Just inside the north doors sits a crypt with Smithson's remains brought from Italy by Alexander Graham Bell. Smithson is the only known person laid to rest on the Mall. The Castle is both a visitor center and the institution's administrative nerve center.

A federally funded quasigovernment agency with over six thousand employees, the Smithsonian receives two-thirds of its budget from Congress. The Smithsonian Board of Regents appoints the Secretary, who leads the institution. The Chief Justice of the Supreme Court serves as Chancellor, and Regents include the Vice President, ex officio; three senators and three congressmen; and nine other notable citizens.

The Smithsonian's many offices and museums offer a constant array of both public programs and exhibitions. To paraphrase Samuel Johnson, when a visitor is tired of the Smithsonian, he is tired of life. Weary of American art? Try Asian or African art. Tired of art? Perhaps fishing cats or prairie dogs, cockroaches or butterflies might interest you. Or gems, or cars, or stamps. You name it, the Smithsonian most likely owns one among its collection of over 137 million artifacts and specimens. Going well beyond its original scientific foundation, the rich breadth of disciplines is simply stunning and all but overwhelming. People from all corners of the world come to visit in a never-ending parade passing through its doors.

I have found no more stimulating work environment than the Smithsonian. One is surrounded by people with curious minds and true devotion. Employee surveys always reveal a deep contentment and a loyalty to the mission. The paramount benefit is the obvious pride that comes from one's role in the stewardship of America's treasures. The employees of the Smithsonian are truly dedicated to their duty to preserve the national collections for future generations. The most rewarding aspect of my job as a museum educator is sharing these treasures with people, helping them understand the stories of the past and nurturing their love of history.

From Biography to Objects

The National Portrait Gallery, one of the smaller museums in the large Smithsonian family of museums, was the perfect place for a young professional to begin a career. Its quiet corridors allowed for reflection that is hard to find in the high-season crowds of the large museums. While I enjoyed working at the Portrait Gallery, my part-time, seasonal job just did not pay the bills. Two years past graduate school I was working several jobs at once and trying to figure out how to break into a full-time history job. No one said it would be easy. I kept reminding myself that some people held museum jobs, and with persistence I could be one of those people.

Determination was, and still is, the key to attaining a museum position. A person seeking to break into museum work must demonstrate perseverance. I was prepared to move almost anywhere in the country, though my preference was to stay on the East Coast. I pictured myself working at a historic site such as Williamsburg. Given the challenging job market, I never expected to stay in Washington, let alone find a permanent position at the Smithsonian, but I did keep an eye on the Smithsonian job listings. Permanent positions at the Portrait Gallery were rare and it looked as if my best chances of finding employment within the Smithsonian were at the National Museum of American History, seven blocks away.

In the fall of 1995, after working at the Portrait Gallery for three years, I noticed a position open at American History. It was thirty-two hours per week with funding for two months. Who would apply for such a position and what did such an odd time period mean? Of course, I had nothing to lose in applying since my Portrait Gallery supervisor was willing to keep me on the roster. I submitted an application for the position of Program Manager of the Hands On History Room (HOHR), a learning center staffed by volunteers. The hiring official, director of education at the museum, hoped the position would be approved for full-time status and eventually become permanent, but there was no guarantee. After what seemed like forever, she called and offered me the job.

The director of education took a risk hiring me. I held a graduate degree in history and had experience working with school groups at the Portrait Gallery, but had never worked with volunteers, knew nothing about education theory, and had never worked at a large museum. I hoped it would turn into a long-term permanent position, but kept a safety net spread at the Portrait Gallery. I somehow managed to work out a deal to split my time between the two museums—four days a week at American History and one day at the Portrait Gallery.

Thus I began a transition from teaching about biography to "material culture," museum jargon for stuff, the objects people leave behind. The American History Museum tells stories of people through its collection of objects. At the Portrait Gallery John Brown's portrait and others taught me that portraits hold great power to convey the essence of the sitter. Objects, I would learn, also hold their own power. Whether their maker or user was famous or not, objects can tell historians and museum visitors a lot about life.

Life in the Attic

That two-month job turned into a six-year stay in "America's attic." Most staff members are not fond of this tag line, yet in some ways it is not altogether farfetched. Say the word "attic," and most imaginations conjure up scenes of a dimly lit, dusty space filled with mysterious boxes overflowing with keepsakes of the past—which inevitably lead to a flood of memories. A visitor's experience at the American History Museum mirrors this scenario. For preservation reasons, its exhibitions have low light levels. Dusting the thousands of objects is a never-ending task, and an observant visitor will often notice a layer of dust on the treasures that are displayed on open platforms. Surprises appear around every corner. A visitor may suddenly come upon the top hat President Lincoln wore the night he was assassinated or a ragged tree stump created by a barrage of bullets on a Civil War battlefield. Winchester, the stuffed horse of Civil War general Philip Sheridan, stands down the corridor from Oscar the Grouch, R2D2, and Mohammed Ali's boxing gloves. A visitor might find his mind wandering back to memories of childhood when he sees the first TV dinner tray or the microphone that Franklin Roosevelt used for fireside chats.

During my time at the Museum I never tired of observing visitors express delight at seeing a familiar object in person. The iconic ruby slippers from *The Wizard of Oz* remain one of the most popular items in the collection. Judy Garland used the museum's pair, one of only four pairs still in existence, for the dance sequences in the film.

Their sequins, though showing wear, still glitter and make young girls gasp in delight. Their enduring popularity is a puzzlement to many museum employees, who become quite good at providing directions to the shoes through gritted teeth and a fake smile. How visitors can place greater importance on the ruby slippers than the Star-Spangled Banner, say, or the first computer, is beyond their comprehension. Apparently even Oprah shares this slipper fascination. When the Museum reopened after being closed over a year for renovation, she invited the museum's director to appear on her show, requesting that he bring along the slippers.

During my years at the Museum, I worked on exhibition teams, trained over 120 volunteers, and began to understand the new medium called the Internet and how it might impact museums. My main responsibility was managing the 60 volunteers who staffed the Hands On History Room, an innovative learning environment and international model of museum education. Tucked into a space on the museum's second floor, the HOHR was an activity-based gallery for all ages. Visitors could gin cotton, send a message in Morse code, make rope, assemble a Chippendale chair, decipher a buffalo hide painting, and try their hand at thirty other assorted activities related to exhibitions throughout the museum. Each activity featured primary source materials and guided visitors in doing rudimentary historical research. The room was a new kind of learning for a traditional history museum where "look but don't touch" was the rule. Staff at natural history museums and science centers had developed discovery rooms where visitors could touch and interact with specimens, but the majority of staff at history museums saw the inclusion of tactile objects as a conflict with their mandate to preserve. History museums relied on labels to convey information.

During my tenure at the American History Museum, I truly began to understand the field of museum education. Museum educators work at the intersection of research and scholarship and the visitor experience. Their main job is to take the content others researched and translate it for many audiences. They display the public face of a museum and shoulder the responsibility of creating and maintaining an informal learning environment where people learn because they want to and not because they have to. My observations of visitors in the Hands On History Room and my careful reading of every comment written in the visitor comment books taught me a great deal about how people interact with history and the value of the experiential environment. I familiarized myself with various education theories and came to recognize that people learn in many different ways. So many people who are hands-on learners or visual learners dislike history museums because they do not enjoy reading labels and are frustrated that their learning preference is not acknowledged.

I'm happy that a transformation has begun in history museums. As more people acknowledge the benefits of addressing various learning preferences, exhibitions have become more accessible and welcoming. They feature mechanical and computer interactives, strong visual and immersive elements, and questioning strategies that engage visitors on multiple levels.

I fondly remember my days in Hands On History as the best possible training ground for a young museum educator. The variety of topics represented allowed me to gain a broad knowledge of American history, provided countless hours of party conversation, and led to projects and adventures I would never have imagined.

5
CONQUERING THE HIGH WHEELER

Get a Bicycle. You will not regret it, if you live.

—*Mark Twain*

People have died riding these things, but I was determined to make the attempt. I stood clumsily gripping a four-foot-two-inch high wheel bicycle, ready to fling my body up onto the seat. There on the National Mall facing the Washington Monument, Smithsonian Castle rising on my left, I was prepared to risk making a fool of myself for this opportunity. Recalling humorist Mark Twain's essay about his own high wheel adventures, I knew the challenges ahead. I envisioned several possible outcomes: a crash, a smooth ride, or running over a small child or dog.

I had wanted to try to ride a high wheeler ever since I started working in the Hands On History Room at the National Museum of American History. Designed to promote active learning, the HOHR featured two attention-grabbing reproduction objects in its large entrance window. Their gleaming frames and large spinning wheels caught the eye of every kid, big and small, daring them to take a ride. There, perched on a platform for all to see—and to ride—stood two high wheel bicycles, great big wheel in the front and small wheel trailing behind.

Perhaps no other objects in the HOHR elicited smiles as much as the high wheelers. As if drawn by some magnetic force, kids would race to them, jump on, and start pedaling. Adults, with a little coaxing, would also climb on and have a grand time—because we had taken risk out of the equation. The bicycles were mounted on rollers, and steel cables held them firmly in place. Security was guaranteed, nothing like the original high wheeler experience. In the 1880s riding a high wheeler was an extreme sport.

High Wheeler History

A high wheeler's alien shape barely hints at its relation to today's bicycles, though our bicycles are its direct descendants. When the word "bicycle" first came into common usage in the 1870s, the term referred to the high wheeler. A decade later, when a new style called safety bicycle came along, most Americans referred to a high wheeler as an "ordinary." The British, with their creative word descriptions, called it a penny farthing, because the ratio of the wheel sizes was similar to that of a penny coin next to a farthing. Today people from most of the British Commonwealth countries still use that term.

The high wheeler craze began in Europe in 1870 and finally jumped the pond in 1876. That year visitors to the Centennial Exposition in Philadelphia saw several English high wheelers on display, and an English racing champion rode his bicycle around the fairgrounds. Americans had seen two-wheeled contraptions before, starting in 1819 with variations over several decades—the velocipede (commonly called the boneshaker) had failed to spark the imaginations of the public and several versions faded from view. High wheelers proved different. One person who noticed them on display in Philadelphia was a Civil War veteran named Albert Pope. Within two years he started a business first importing and then manufacturing bicycles near his home in Boston. His company debuted its popular Columbia model in 1878. The "cult of the ordinary" quickly took root in Boston, home of the first American bicycle club, and spread around the country. A year later Washington DC, Philadelphia, Brooklyn, and Chicago all started clubs.

What spell did this machine cast on people of all ages? Why would they endanger life and limb to ride the wheels? In an era when travel by land was defined by trains and horsepower, the high wheeler represented the freedom of the open road. Bicycles were a fast and relatively inexpensive form of personal transport that brought a newfound independence. In the advertisements for his Columbia bicycle, Pope described the high wheeler as "an ever-saddled horse which eats nothing."

Yet every new invention draws its share of critics. While young men reveled in the freedom and adventure bicycles provided, other reactions were not so complimentary. The machines threatened the status quo in a world firmly rooted in horse culture. Some critics gave the pejorative term "scorcher" to bicyclists who rode by carriages at great speeds, scaring the horses. "Cads on castors" described the bicyclists who dared to disrupt the domain of the horse. As more and more bicyclists took to the road on Sundays—the only day off for most working people—they often skipped church. This supposedly prompted one minister to condemn the high wheeler, saying that the road of the cyclists leads to a place where there is no mud on the streets because of its high temperatures. His disapproval sought to put the fear of hell itself into the wheelmen.

Women did not want to sit by and let the men have all the fun. They cast aside their corsets and began sporting bloomers that allowed freer movement. While some physicians cautioned against bicycling and its possible dangers to feminine health, this did not stop many determined women. Mrs. Harriette Mills of Washington

DC formed the country's first women's bicycle club in 1888, and club members began riding a new form of bicycle with lower wheels.

Early bicycles represented adventure, but also danger. Imagine: you're perched up on the seat at the height of a man's shoulders. Most roads at the time are little more than dirt or gravel, with unexpected ruts and surprises around every bend. You suddenly see a large rock in your path. It's too late to swerve around it. You sit precariously, your center of gravity tilted forward. Your only way to stop, short of crashing, is the rudimentary cup brake located at twelve o'clock on the wheel, directly in front of the handlebars. The more pressure applied to the brake lever, the quicker the stop. However, since there are no gears, you can't coast to a stop. A touch of the brake to the solid rubber tire causes the bike to slow. Touch the brake a tad too firmly, and you are suddenly taking a "header," flying headfirst over the handlebars, wondering if you will survive.

An elderly visitor to the Hands On History Room told me he owed his existence to the high wheeler. He explained that his father had raced high wheelers and once took a header and was knocked unconscious. When he opened his eyes, he was staring up into the angelic face of a nurse. They fell in love, got married, and had a baby.

In 1879 about twenty-five hundred people purchased bicycles in the United States, and the number increased every year. Three years later Pope's shop produced one thousand sets of wheels per month, and new bicycle clubs sprouted across the country. But their eager members faced growing conflicts with local jurisdictions that banned bicycles from park trails and other roads under pressure from the horse-and-carriage crowd. Pope and others launched the League of American Wheelmen in 1880 to lobby for the rights of its members. The group eventually spearheaded the Good Roads movement, an attempt to improve American roads.

In the early 1880s, when the high wheeler was at peak popularity in America, humorist Mark Twain learned to ride one. He later wrote an article about his attempts, entitled "Taming the Bicycle." His advice: "Get a bicycle. You will not regret it, if you live." Mark

Twain rode a fifty-inch high wheeler, or "graceful cobweb," as he called it. *Graceful?* Perched four feet off the ground, the rider of a high wheeler must conquer more than a few anxieties in order to ride.

My Desire to Ride

Like Twain, I felt the allure of the bike and wondered at the skills and courage required to master one. I conducted yearly training for the HOHR volunteers about the history of high wheelers and about the practicality of riding them. I answered countless questions from volunteers and visitors alike about how a person got on and off the wheels without breaking his neck, secretly wishing that I could speak from experience. Our high wheelers required absolutely no balance, and a stool and ample step attached to the frames guaranteed an easy ascent for visitors of all sizes and girths.

I plotted how I might someday give one a try and began to imagine a plan: one night, when no one was around, I would take the bike off its track and out into the museum's central corridor. I would easily mount the bike and glide across the second floor, to the first ladies' gowns and past the Star-Spangled Banner. The realist in me could imagine my jaunt ending with the crash of Plexiglas as I rode the thing into one of the exhibition cases—or worse, ran over Jacqueline Kennedy's gown and became entangled in it—or even worse yet, cracked my skull on Horatio Greenough's giant white marble statue of George Washington seated as a Greek god.

Years went by and I wondered if I would ever get the opportunity to ride. Finally, my chance came one beautiful day in May. The museum held a program about bicycles, and the Potomac Wheelmen, a group from Maryland that rides antique high wheelers, came to demonstrate their machines. In preliminary talks before the event, I had carefully hinted to one of the members that I really wanted to try riding one and was determined not to miss this opportunity. Surely, it could be arranged.

After lectures and demonstrations, the program concluded with a grand parade of bikes down the National Mall, a sight to behold. With the red sandstone turrets of the Smithsonian Castle towering in the background, the scene could have been direct from 1880s Washington. Bicycles of various shapes and sizes ridden by men and women in late-nineteenth-century dress slowly moved down the Mall.

As the parade ended there were butterflies flying around in my stomach. One owner had graciously offered to let me try out his wheels after the parade. Now was my moment. I knew exactly how to mount and dismount, but putting that book knowledge into practice was another story. The ultimate skill in riding a high wheeler is tested at those moments of embarking and disembarking. Heart racing, I stood behind the fifty-inch-high big wheel and made my first attempt. I put my left foot on the narrow step, pushed off, and got the bicycle moving with my right foot. I quickly realized that the loose gravel of the Mall's paths was hardly the ideal spot for a novice. Then again, if I wanted historical accuracy, this was it.

I recalled Mark Twain's efforts and his description of how to mount a high wheeler: "When you have reached the point in bicycling where you can balance the machine tolerably fairly and propel it and steer it, then comes your next task—how to mount it. You do it in this way: you hop along behind it on your right foot, resting the other on the mounting-peg, and grasping the tiller with your hands. At the word, you rise on the peg, stiffen your left leg, hang your other one around in the air in a general indefinite way, lean your stomach against the rear of the saddle, and then fall off, maybe on one side, maybe on the other; but you fall off. You get up and do it again; and once more; and then several times." *Maybe I should be wearing kneepads and wrist guards*, I thought as I walked the bike to the flat cement terrace surrounding the museum. Certainly this would be a better place. There, on smooth pavement, I tried again. Standing behind the bike, with one foot on the mounting step attached to the frame, I pushed off and carefully balanced, gingerly moving my body up and onto the seat. The next second I was riding through the warm air, high above the museum visitors nearby. A feeling of elation swept over me. I had done it, without falling.

While I didn't want to draw attention, there was no way to avoid it. Riding a high wheeler in the 1990s was a spectacle just as it had been one hundred years earlier. I thought of the description written by bicyclist Karl Kron in 1882.

> When the solitary wayfarer glides through the country on top of a bicycle his relations to his human environment are absolutely altered. Mounted on a four-foot wheel, which sends him spinning swiftly and noiselessly o'er hill and dale, the whilom tramp is transformed into a personage of consequence and attractiveness. He becomes at once a notable feature in the landscape, drawing to himself the gaze . . . of all whose eyes are there to see. His fellow humans ignore or avoid him no longer. Gentle or simple, they all recognize in him the representative of something novel and remarkable. He is the center of universal curiosity and comment. His presence illustrates a fresh triumph of mind over matter. All creatures who ever walked have wished that they might fly, and here is a flesh-and-blood man who can really hitch wings to his feet.

I barely breathed as I rounded the turns, thinking that somehow movement caused by breathing would throw me off-balance. Around the building once, then twice, past the Delaware flag, the Pennsylvania flag, and the flags of all fifty states. I cautiously steered around visitors, praying no one would dart in front of me. Lacking a big horn to honk, I yelled out "Excuse me!" to anyone in my path. Stories of spectacular crashes swirled in my mind. The *Washington Post* headline would read, "Smithsonian Staff Member Killed in High Wheeler Crash at the American History Museum," or worse, "Man Taught Many to Ride, But Could Not Do It Himself."

The dangers of riding a high wheeler, while downplayed by most cycling magazines of the period, were sometimes outlined in stark terms. An article from the late 1870s stated: "When a man is riding a bicycle he looks neither to the right nor to the left, but appears to be gazing about five hundred yards into futurity, as if trying to solve the problems of the hereafterness of the unknowableness of the unknowable hereafter. He is not, however. He is simply wondering, in case of a sudden header [flying headfirst over the handlebars], whether his skull would be split open wide, or if he would escape with his nose mashed all over his face."

After three laps around the museum, I decided it was time to end the adventure. However, as I began to think about dismounting, fear set in. I was four feet off the ground moving forward. I couldn't coast to a stop; there were no gears or chain. The expert riders sometimes swung a leg to one side and rode the pedals to a stop. Others slowed the wheel with the brake and jumped off. However, these options took a bit of coordination, and at the moment I was not feeling very coordinated. I could maybe jump off as it fell over, but I didn't think that option would prove very graceful. What did Twain do? "And now you come to the voluntary dismount; you learned the other kind first of all. It is quite easy to tell one how to do the voluntary dismount; the words are few, the requirement simple, and apparently undifficult; let your left pedal go down till your left leg is nearly straight, turn your wheel to the left, and get off as you would from a horse. It certainly does sound exceedingly easy; but it isn't. I don't know why it isn't but it isn't. Try as you may, you don't get down as you would from a horse, you get down as you would from a house afire. You make a spectacle of yourself every time." Twain had crashed into a horse pulling a wagon of cabbages.

If the bike's owner wasn't nervous for his wheels before this, perhaps now he saw the look of terror creeping into my eyes. He certainly didn't want his beautiful bicycle to end up a mound of twisted metal. So, as he ran along beside me, I admitted my awkward situation and he came to my rescue. I slowed and he grabbed the bike and steadied it while I climbed down under the observation of a small crowd of visitors. So in the end I cheated in the dismount— not that people from the past didn't cheat. Anything is fair to avoid the spectacle of a crash.

I had done it! Now I could proudly say I'd ridden a high wheeler and survived. From that day on I enjoyed the look of awe I received when museum visitors and docents heard of my riding experience.

Other High Wheel Adventurers

My ride gave me a new appreciation for those intrepid riders of the past, especially Thomas Stevens, a young man who was one of the grandest of adventure seekers. I am not convinced Stevens fully grasped what he was getting himself into when at eight o'clock on the morning of April 22, 1884, he set out on his fifty-inch Columbia Expert for a ride around the world.

The twenty-nine-year-old Englishman started in San Francisco and traveled east, ending 13,500 miles later in December 1886 in Yokohama, Japan. His 1888 book, *Around the World on a Penny-Farthing*, describes his experiences, from teaching a Persian prince to ride to using his bike to pole vault over countless small stream beds. During his journey across the States, members of various cycling clubs would sometimes join him. In Wyoming, the members of the Laramie Bicycle Club were the first wheelmen to support his trip.

Stevens met all kinds of interesting people and rode wherever he could find a decent path. In New York State he met "a physician who uses the wheel in preference to a horse, in making professional calls throughout the surrounding country." Often, especially out west, it was easiest to ride the railroad tracks. In New York he rode the towpath of the Erie Canal. "The greatest drawback to peaceful cycling is the towing-mule and his unwarrantable animosity toward the bicycle, and the awful, unmentionable profanity engendered thereby in the utterances of the boatmen."

Each day presented its own challenges. "I consider it a lucky day that passes without adding one or more to my long and eventful list of headers, and to-day I am fairly 'unhorsed' by a squall of wind that—taking me unawares—blows me and the bicycle fairly over." However, in England, Stevens was impressed when he realized that he traveled three hundred miles without taking one header—a record thus far on his journey.

Thomas Stevens was the first and only person to ride a high wheeler around the world. For those of us wheelmen who have tamed the high wheeler, that's an awe-inspiring feat. He was not, however, noted among the daredevil high wheelers of the age.

In my opinion, some of the craziest adventure seekers were those who dared speed down the carriage road from the 6,288 foot summit of Mount Washington, the highest of the White Mountains in New Hampshire. The paved road, completed in 1861, was 16 feet wide and about 7.5 miles long, with a vertical drop of 4,000 feet. With an average grade of 12 percent and a maximum of 26 percent, its 99 curves quickly lured the most fearless wheelmen. The first recorded descent, by E. H. Corson of Rochester, New Hampshire, took 90 minutes. Yes, on a high wheeler 5 feet off the ground with a simple spoon brake at the top of the big wheel. Two weeks later, a Massachusetts man lowered the record by ten minutes. A year later, three St. Louis wheelmen made the trip. One of the three set the record of fifty-one minutes. Success came with a score of thirty-one headers between them, but no broken bones.

The high wheeler era lasted only through the 1880s. The greater consumer market still reacted with hesitancy toward the potential dangers of the high wheel. *Bicycling World*, a weekly newsletter, declared that "many a hardy and skillful bicyclist has been seriously and permanently injured by a forward fall off a high mount." Its conclusion: the need for safer bicycles, so that a larger ridership would not be deterred.

Fortunately, a man named John Kemp Starley invented a new style of cycle in 1885. The safety bicycle featured a lower frame, pneumatic tires, a better braking system, and a chain. Because bicycle manufacturers saw the potential of new sales with older and less courageous riders, they soon recognized safety bicycles as the next trend. Thus, the heyday of the high wheeler lasted only fifteen years or so.

We are fortunate that Mark Twain and Thomas Stevens lived to write about their experiences with a high wheeler. I sometimes wish they could witness today's bicycles, equipment, and races. Would they think our cycles are too easy to ride or would they consider us the luckiest of riders to live in an age of advanced bicycle technology? As for Thomas Stevens, he would probably move on to bungee jumping.

6
DOES THIS MAKE COTTON OR GIN?

[O]ne of our great embarrassments is the clearing
the cotton of the seed. I feel a considerable interest
in the success of your invention, for family use.

—*Thomas Jefferson to Eli Whitney, 1793*

Growing up a Yankee in Pennsylvania I saw fields of tobacco, corn, and alfalfa, but never cotton. On a late fall visit to southeastern Virginia, I remember standing captivated by my first sight of a mature cotton field, white fiber dripping from dried bolls. Little did I know that in the future I would raise my own cotton patch on the National Mall in Washington and become intimately acquainted with cotton gins. Before I worked at the National Museum of American History I was confident in the knowledge that Eli Whitney invented the cotton gin. One day this seemingly black-and-white fact suddenly became gray.

The Hands On History Gin

With a roar of well-oiled parts, the hand-cranked reproduction cotton gin in the Hands On History Room drew lots of attention. On busy days visitors kept the gin in constant motion, and the steady whirring of gears continued for hours. As a tool for teaching history, the gin was ideal. By turning a crank, visitors could immediately understand why Eli Whitney's gin transformed cotton production in the South, making it easy to separate the seeds from the fiber.

Visitors would first grab a handful of raw short-fibered cotton and feel how the seeds are deeply embedded in the soft threads. After trying to pick several from the fiber, a procedure sometimes called finger ginning, visitors understood the dilemma: processing short-fibered cotton by hand requires a lot of effort. As a result, the cotton gin seems like a magic trick. Put a little cotton in the gin's receptacle, turn the crank, and watch. The crankshaft turns the gears, which rotate two cylinders. The raw cotton tumbles over a cylinder with circular saw blades. The teeth cut the seeds from the fiber and an opposing cylinder with wire brushes picks it up, sending the seeds to one receptacle and fluffy seedless cotton fiber to another. At this point I could see the virtual light bulb going off in visitors' heads. "*This* is how the cotton gin works . . . I read about it so long ago in history class and never really understood it until now," they marveled.

In reality the cotton gin was the bane of the staff's existence. Despite its sturdy metal gears, it proved a delicate and temperamental machine. One small seed in a gear's teeth could cause major problems. If a visitor accidentally put already ginned cotton through the machine instead of raw cotton, more damage could result. It required constant monitoring, yet, despite its noise and dust, the gin was beloved by most of the volunteers who worked in the HOHR. When it broke down, they couldn't wait for its return. They loved its ability to prompt so many interesting discussions with visitors. Older Southerners told of picking cotton as a child, of dragging long canvas bags for hours through rows of cotton and of tender hands ripped by the sharp bolls. Some spoke of piles of cotton seeds and presses that squeezed them into oil. We all had favorite visitor stories. One of mine was the day a very serious woman walked up to the machine clearly labeled "Cotton Gin" and asked in a loud voice, "So what does this thing make, cotton or gin?"

A Cotton-Picking Experiment

One year I had an idea. Many visitors at the gin questioned how cotton grows and what the plants look like. A brief but disastrous attempt to grow cotton plants in the HOHR with artificial light had failed years earlier. But what about planting a patch outside? Would cotton grow in Washington DC? A meeting with the Smithsonian horticultural staff ended with their promise of a roughly twelve-by-twenty-foot cotton patch just outside of the museum's Mall entrance on the terrace the following spring. We would experiment.

That spring the gardeners placed about thirty small plants into the loose soil. With great excitement I watched as the spindly ten-inch plants quickly grew, enjoying the warm sunshine. By early July the now attractive plants were filled with three-inch-wide pink blossoms. A tiny seed pod called a boll soon developed from each blossom, and by late summer I began counting the number of bolls on each plant. If they all reached maturity, we could expect a healthy harvest. By August the two-foot-high plants were thriving in the heat and humidity of the Washington summer. However, we soon learned that despite our urban location, we needed to prepare for battle. The squirrels, rabbits, rats, and birds of the neighborhood had somehow recognized a new source of food. I marveled at the fact that a rat or squirrel that lived its entire life within a few blocks of the museum and had never seen a cotton plant before, knew instinctively that a boll might make a tasty treat. A short chicken wire fence kept a few critters out, but we needed to get creative. At one point we tried putting human hair around the plants, having heard that squirrels do not like the texture of hair.

We lost the battle that first summer, but the following year a good-sized crop reached maturity, much to my delight. In early September the ultimate hands-on activity was about to commence. I had read oral histories describing the process of picking cotton by hand. The reminiscences spanned the spectrum from nostalgic annual community social event to forced back-breaking slave labor. John Earl Little of New Albany, Mississippi, began picking cotton at age six in the mid-1950s. His family picked cotton from the end of July until the end of September and earned two or three dollars for every 100 pounds they picked. A person could pick 200–250 pounds a day. Youngsters enduring the drudgery of twelve-hour days found ways to create some fun. Little described cotton-boll fights, throwing immature hard green cotton bolls that hadn't opened at a friend's head.

Solomon Northup offered a different perspective, one that more accurately represents the grueling nature of picking cotton for hundreds of thousands of people throughout American history. Born a free black in the North, he was kidnapped in Washington in 1841 and taken to a cotton plantation in Louisiana. After twelve years in slavery he was rescued and wrote a book about his experiences. He described his days of picking cotton:

> One morning, long before I was in a proper condition to labor, Epps [his master] appeared at the cabin door, and, presenting me a sack, ordered me to the cotton field. At this time I had had no experience whatever in cotton picking. It was an awkward business indeed. While, others used both hands, snatching the cotton and depositing it in the mouth of the sack, with a precision and dexterity that was incomprehensible to me, I had to seize the boll with one hand, and deliberately draw out the white, gushing blossom with the other.
>
> Depositing the cotton in the sack, moreover, was a difficulty that demanded the exercise of both hand and eyes. I was compelled to pick it from the ground where it would fall, nearly as often as from the stalk where it had grown. I made havoc also with the branches, loaded with the yet unbroken bolls, the long, cumbersome sack swinging from side to side in a manner not allowable in the cotton field. After a most laborious day I arrived at the gin-house with my load. When the scale determined its weight to be only ninety-five pounds, not half the quantity required of the poorest picker, Epps threatened the severest

flogging, but in consideration of my being a "raw hand," concluded to pardon me on that occasion. The following day, and many days succeeding, I returned at night with no better success—I was evidently not designed for that kind of labor. I had not the gift—the dexterous fingers and quick motion of Patsey, who could fly along one side of a row of cotton, stripping it of its undefiled and fleecy whiteness miraculously fast. Practice and whipping were alike unavailing, and Epps, satisfied of it at last, swore I was a disgrace—that I was not fit to associate with a cotton-picking "nigger"—that I could not pick enough in a day to pay the trouble of weighing it, and that I should go into the cotton field no more.

Museum staff decided to harvest our crop in front of visitors. Every few days I encouraged the volunteers to join me in the cotton patch. A crowd circled us as we gingerly tore the fiber from the bolls, in full view of the Washington Monument. Under no pressure for high productivity, we could take our time and prevent stabbing our fingers on the bolls. The experience proved a great teaching moment for those visitors who were lucky enough to watch the picking and then gin the product of our toil.

Often young visitors would ask if they could keep some seeds. We sent many little plastic baggies of ginned cotton and seeds home with eager cotton farmers, unsure if the seeds would germinate. Our raw cotton was donated by a ginning facility in eastern North Carolina and arrived in a large bale. We had to freeze it to kill any pests hiding in the fibers, since the last thing we wanted was fiber-chewing insects invading the national collections. A return visitor finally confirmed that his HOHR seeds had successfully sprouted. For all I know, somewhere out there someone might still be growing cotton from seeds they took from the Hands On History Room.

A Twist to the Story

History stories may seem straightforward . . . but one thing that fascinates me about the past is that there's always more to the story. Among the iconic objects in the American History Museum's collections is a courtroom model of Eli Whitney's cotton gin built around 1845 to defend Whitney's patent during an infringement claim. Eli Whitney occupies a revered place in the pantheon of American inventors. His profile is one of four medallion plaster portraits of inventors set into the walls of the Great Hall of the National Portrait Gallery, originally the United States Patent Office Building.

According to the popular story, eighteenth-century planters on the Sea Islands off the coast of South Carolina grew long-staple cotton, the variety with long glossy fibers. The smooth black seeds embedded in the fibers are relatively easy to remove. However, the plant's growing range was limited to a narrow sliver of coastal land. Another kind of cotton, short-staple cotton, has shorter fibers, and grows inland. But its fuzzy greenish seeds stick in the fiber and are much harder to remove. Cultivation of this cotton would not be profitable because of the labor involved. Most American students learn that in 1793 Eli Whitney invented the cotton gin, which successfully removed the seeds from short-staple cotton. The machine transformed the agricultural South as cotton quickly became a profitable crop across the southern United States. Harvesting the plant remained labor intensive, and thus slave labor followed the gin. The connection between the cotton gin and slavery is engrained in public consciousness.

Given this story, two implications might seem obvious: first, before Mr. Whitney's gin, people cultivating cotton around the world separated the seeds and fiber by hand, and second, prior to Whitney's invention the British textile manufacturers relied on cotton ginned by hand. Yet these assumptions are wrong.

One day a new story rocked our secure cotton ginning world. Along came Angela Lakwete, a Johns Hopkins University postdoctoral fellow at the museum. A textiles conservator, Angela was in the middle of researching and writing a book about the history of cotton ginning. She presented her research and explained that for millennia prior to Whitney, cotton-producing cultures around the world were using something called a roller gin to remove seeds from cotton. What? Cotton gins before Eli Whitney? But, indeed, historical fact shows that cotton gins have been used in some form or another since the first century.

It turns out that short-staple (upland) cotton, the kind with the fuzzy seeds, is the dominant species on the globe. Late-nineteenth-century British botanist Sir George Watt wrote that British colonists around the world grew short-staple cotton, the principal import of the British textile industry. Gins incorporating rollers existed for millennia on every continent where cotton grew. Powered by humans, animals, or water, the gins processed cotton until the last decade of the 1700s, when the demand for cotton outweighed the production capacity of the roller gin. Textile manufacturers demanded that the British Board of Trade offer financial incentives to inventors to encourage the invention of a gin that would increase the production of ginned cotton beyond that of the traditional roller gins.

Further examination of the Whitney interpretation raises several questions. Did American farmers who grew long-staple cotton use these roller gins? What then was special about Whitney's gin? The ultimate question formed in my mind. Was Whitney getting just a little bit too much credit in American textbooks? Did he invent *the* cotton gin or *a* cotton gin? Angela's answer was a resounding yes to the former and "a" to the latter.

Building a Gin

Angela's research provided a much more layered and complex story. We decided that the museum's visitors deserved to know this broader context and applied for a grant to expand the story told in the Hands On History Room. A roller gin sitting beside the Whitney-inspired gin would offer visitors a hands-on comparison. We would test for ourselves whether or not using a roller gin would work with short-staple cotton. With the Lemelson Center for the Study of Invention and Innovation's offer of support, we began the search for the right person to build our gin. Who in America had experience constructing hand-cranked wooden roller gins? We decided to ask our existing gin's builder, a mechanic in the Shenandoah Valley of Virginia, to take a stab at the project, and he eagerly accepted the challenge.

Angela gathered together a collection of blueprints of early roller gins with help from the United States Department of Agriculture's Southwest Cotton Ginning Research Laboratory in New Mexico. Staff there prepared a full set of technical drawings and photos of an Indian roller gin from their collection. We also looked at several roller gins from other countries that were part of the American History Museum's textile collection. While mostly based on the gin in the USDA collection, our gin would eventually include the best features of several gins.

We ended up with something that looked like a wooden wash wringer. Angela described it this way: "The roller gin consisted of two rollers, one placed over the other. They were secured in an upright wooden frame, the size typically dependent on the power source. Wedges in the uprights squeezed the two rollers tightly together while bearings allowed them to rotate freely. The rollers were turned in opposite directions by means of a universal screw or by cranks mounted on each of the rollers." While the concept of squeezing cotton through two rollers seems simple enough, figuring out the best length for the rollers and getting the correct tension on them proved quite difficult.

Once the gin was finished, our next challenge was learning how to use it. Angela's thesis posited that roller gins required much more skill from the operator than other gins. She was adamant that we needed to find someone skilled in the process who could test our gin and teach us the correct ginning technique. Searching far and wide she somehow found Mr. Zafar Khalid, who lived in California. Mr. Khalid had learned the skill of roller ginning during his childhood in Pakistan. We would bring him to Washington to teach us.

The day he arrived we nervously showed him our new roller gin and invited him to give it a try. He took a handful of cotton and pulled it apart with his fingers to get rid of any clumps. He then spread it along the rollers and held it there with one hand while turning the crank with the other. He gently fed the fibers into the turning rollers, which sucked the cotton through, leaving the seeds to drop. It looked so easy. When it was my turn, I tried to follow his lead. The cotton bunched up and jammed the rollers. I quickly learned firsthand that there is skill involved in roller ginning. We ginned both long-staple and short-staple cotton that day. The gin easily removed the black seeds from the long fiber and the fuzzy seeds from the short fiber. Mr. Khalid confirmed that growing up, he had ginned short-fibered cotton. Angela was right, of course. Roller gins could gin short-staple cotton.

Living in California and working in computer technology, Mr. Khalid was worlds removed from his childhood in Pakistan. But this project brought back memories, and prior to his visit to Washington, he had traveled to Pakistan to see family. While there, he had purchased two roller gins, which he brought to show us. They were small dark wooden gins with ornate carving. Both had seen years of use but worked quite well. He donated one to the museum's collection, and Angela eagerly purchased the other one. It proved to be a fulfilling cross-cultural journey that none of us had expected when we started the project. A fifty-something-year-old man from Pakistan had traveled several thousand miles from California to help the Smithsonian learn about cotton ginning.

Giving Credit Where It Is Due

What was unique about Whitney's gin? His patent application included this description: "The cotton gin cranked cotton through rollers with teeth made of wire. The wire teeth tore the green seeds from the cotton. Iron slits let the cotton pass through, but not the seeds. A second rotating cylinder of bristles removed the seedless cotton from the wires. Through a simple arrangement of belts, the same crank turned both the cylinder with wires and another smaller one with bristles." He identified five principal parts of his gin, and these essential elements have not changed in the two hundred years since. Whitney's gin represented a dramatic shift in the idea of how to separate cotton seeds from the fiber.

At the end of his life, Whitney claimed that his idea was entirely original. Even earlier, in a 1793 letter to Thomas Jefferson, he had written that "it is entirely new and constructed in a different manner and upon different principles from any other Cotton Gin or Machine heretofore known or used for that purpose." Angela concluded that he had based it on the rollers of the roller gin, and she identified his paradigm-shifting innovation to be the breastwork through which the teeth passed. But it comes as no surprise that people have accused Whitney of borrowing ideas from African American slaves or Catherine Greene, widow of Revolutionary War hero Nathanael Greene. Whitney was a guest on Greene's plantation near Savannah, Georgia, where he heard local planters talk about the challenge of trying to separate seeds from short-staple cotton. Some people think he saw slaves experimenting with methods to gin this cotton and adapted their ideas. Other people think Catherine herself inspired Whitney. One article recounted how her action of picking up a hearth brush in front of Whitney helped him solve the problem of removing the cotton fiber from the wire teeth.

On October 15, 1793, Whitney sent Secretary of State Thomas Jefferson his patent application, writing, "It has been my endeavor to give a precise idea of every part of the machine, and if I have failed in elegance, I hope I have not been deficient in point of accuracy." Jefferson responded the following month that he had received Whitney's drawing, but still needed a working model. Jefferson also expressed a personal interest in the invention: "The State of Virginia, of which I am, carries on household manufactures of cotton to a great extent, as I also do myself, and one of our great embarrassments is the cleaning the cotton of the seed. I feel considerable interest in the success of your invention for family use." Whitney received his patent award the next year.

But in 1796 a Georgia mechanic named Hodgen Holmes patented a saw gin, which essentially cut the seeds out of the fiber. He replaced the wired cylinder of Whitney's gin with circular saws. Whitney's business partner, Phineas Miller, sued Holmes for infringement and successfully managed to have his patent voided. He then claimed that the idea for the saw gin was Whitney's idea from the beginning. These are the stories students don't read in the history textbooks.

British manufacturers initially rejected cotton processed by both the wire and saw gins because they viewed its quality inferior—the fiber was not uniform in length and was shorter than that ginned with the roller gin. Angela's research revealed that "only after two decades of social and technical mediation did textile manufacturers, by then both British and American, capitulate to the low quality of cotton fiber delivered by the new gins. The quantities of fiber that the toothed gins produced and the subsequent lower price induced textile manufacturers to make changes in their own equipment in order to use it." So quantity won out over quality, and cotton production rapidly spread throughout the South.

The 1860 Agricultural Census recorded a cotton harvest of 5,387,052 bales weighing 400 pounds each. Cotton had become a key block in the foundation of the Southern economy—prompting rhetoric such as that from South Carolina governor James Hammond: "You dare not make war upon cotton; no power on earth dare to make war upon it. Cotton is king."

The National Museum of American History began to tell visitors a new story. Eli Whitney invented *a* type of cotton gin—not *the* cotton gin—and received the first U.S. patent for a gin. Unfortunately, spreading a new interpretation of history is hard work, and while thousands of people who visited the Hands On History Room learned this added context, few if any American history books today tell the broader story. Historians in other parts of the world understand that the cotton gin was not invented in America. And Angela Lakwete published her book, which makes a valiant attempt to correct the historical record.

This project demonstrates both the complexity of historical interpretation and the reality that historical fact changes based on historical evidence and perspective. These days if the topic of cotton comes up at a party, beware! I unleash a torrent of knowledge about cotton gins. I can't help myself. My friends stand stunned as I attempt to enlighten them on the fascinating history of this invention. They have no idea that this Northerner has picked and ginned cotton and even guided the construction of a gin. "Gin," by the way, is a contraction for the word "ingenuity" or "engine" and originally meant a clever way of doing something. Today it's a machine that separates the seed from the fiber.

And for the record, it doesn't make cotton *or* gin.

7
MARY, NOT BETSY

'Tis the star-spangled banner—O long may it wave
O'er the land of the free and the home of the brave!

—*Francis Scott Key*

The saying that all politics is local could easily be applied to history. Having worked at three national museums, I understand that America's story is really many smaller stories. History is a collection of stories like the quilt squares on a colorful and intricately patterned bed covering. Each square represents the people and events that have formed a larger pattern. The U.S. quilt contains squares of events and people—well known and unknown—pieced together to form a large tapestry of national experience. Some stories are tragic and some are triumphant, most are based on fact, and a few are cherished myths. At the center of America's quilt are the stories of the men and women who founded our country.

In any Fourth of July parade marching down an American street, you will no doubt see people dressed as George Washington, Thomas Jefferson, Benjamin Franklin, and other founding fathers. Along with these gentlemen often sits a woman in colonial costume, a mobcap on her head and a thirteen-star American flag draped over her knee. Most American children know her by name.

Americans identify Betsy Ross as the woman who sewed America's first stars and stripes. You can visit her restored house several blocks from Independence Hall in Philadelphia. But the story linking Betsy Ross to the first flag is one of our cherished *myths*. Historians can find no definitive documentary evidence to support the story that Betsy sewed the first flag at the request of General Washington. Yes, she was a well-known seamstress in Philadelphia at that time, and she knew various members of Congress. Yes, she sewed flags. But the crucial link to this notable first, a solid piece of historical evidence, is missing. If she were alive today, she would likely be surprised to hear her story. Historians credit her grandson, William Canby, with manufacturing the legend in 1870. Unfortunately Mary Pickersgill, another seamstress from Philadelphia, didn't have a grandson quite as keen on marketing the memory of his grandmother.

A Jewel in the Crown

One of my projects at the National Museum of American History drew me into the world of Mary Pickersgill, whose name has been lost in popular history. "Lost" is perhaps the wrong word because it is doubtful she was ever included in history books. Yet today her restored house in Baltimore is a museum called the Flag House— because Mary sewed the Star-Spangled Banner.

The actual flag, subject of the U.S. national anthem, now belongs to the American people. One of the jewels in the Smithsonian crown, this textile is arguably one of America's most valuable treasures. The National Museum of American History, where it resides, was designed with a specific place at its center to display the huge thirty-by-thirty-four-foot flag. From opening day in 1964 through the museum's first three decades, the flag hung in Flag Hall at the very middle of the building and greeted every visitor entering from the National Mall. Though it was kept in low light, the wear of time took its toll. Inspection showed the need for a major conservation project to secure the flag's future.

Therefore in December 1998 the museum lowered the flag one last time. Staff members experienced a rare opportunity to get up close and examine this national icon. I remember putting my face within a foot of the fibers and feeling two distinct emotions: awe from the power of this historic object imbued with symbolism and shock at the flag's worn condition. Away from the painted backdrop, its fragile state was starkly evident. In many sections, only a few fibers remained. Without a doubt, now was the last chance to save this significant piece of American history.

Conservation work done on the flag over the years included careful vacuuming to remove dust buildup. This latest major conservation project would supersede all others, with a price tag of over $10 million, which was generously donated by several funders. Beyond cleaning and repairing the flag, staff would eventually preserve it in a brand-new state-of-the-art display. As part of the first phase of the project, the museum's administration decided to build a conservation lab with a glass wall so visitors could watch the work in progress. One reason may have been the donor's stipulation in 1913 that "any American citizen who visits the museum with the expectation of seeing the flag be sure of finding it in its accustomed place." Admittedly there was some chuckling among the staff when this announcement was made, because the tedious work of conservation is not particularly exciting to observers. Certainly not like watching zoo keepers feed the pandas.

The observation area proved a successful venture. Visitors were treated with a behind-the-scenes look at the Smithsonian. Here they could look through a fifty-foot-long glass wall and watch conservators lying on their stomachs over the flag on a specially made gantry, carefully snipping approximately 1.7 million stitches to separate the flag from a linen backing dating back to 1914. Using a camera attached to a microscope, the conservators documented the condition of each square inch of the flag, noting stains and fiber deterioration. The next step involved using dry sponges to blot surface dirt, mostly carbon and oily residues, from the fragile fibers. Next, they attempted to clean all embedded dirt using a mixture of acetone and water. Finally the conservators sewed the delicate fibers to a new backing of Stabiltex, a lightweight polyester material. All the while, visitors learned about the care that goes into preserving America's treasures.

The staff created a small exhibition to supplement the conservation work. As the Education Department looked for additional ways to teach visitors about the flag, staff in the Hands On Science Center developed a hands-on activity focused on conservation. Visitors could perform various burn tests on swatches of wool, cotton, and synthetic materials to determine substance and durability based on smell and burn rate. Likewise, staff decided an activity focusing on the history of the flag should be added to the Hands On History Room. As program manager of the HOHR, I took the challenge.

What Story to Tell?

I decided to focus the activity on ages eight and above. My rather vague objective was to help visitors learn about the flag's history. What story should I explore? I solicited ideas from colleagues—everything from visitors designing a flag to sewing a giant flag. Yet I kept looking for inspiration. What would interest visitors and reel them in for a personal connection?

The Stars and Stripes is a powerful visual representation of the ideals Americans cherish. Throughout American history wartime has usually brought revived patriotic attachment to the flag. During the Civil War and World War II the flag was a strong symbol of national identity. The 1960s was a decade of unrest and contested values. Flag burning became a powerful statement of protest and in 1968 Congress passed the Federal Flag Desecration Law, making it illegal to publicly mutilate, deface, defile, burn, or trample upon the American flag. A year later, with the world watching on TV, astronauts planted a flag on the Moon, creating perhaps one of the most iconic images of the flag. On a visit to the museum in 1998, President Bill Clinton said, "This Star-Spangled Banner and all its successors have come to embody our country, what we think of as America." Few citizens of other countries wear their flag as a fashion statement—from political lapel pins to expensive sweaters. We Americans literally wear our patriotism on our sleeves. We are as patriotic a bunch of people as any on earth. Nothing inspires the soul of most Americans like the sight of our flag flying in a stiff breeze while the national anthem plays.

Rarely is an object such as a flag the centerpiece of a broad national story. However, the flag, the inspiration for America's national anthem, holds a revered place in the hearts of Americans. Still, a quick audience survey confirmed that most Americans haven't a clue what they are singing about when they sing the anthem. They know Francis Scott Key wrote the song lyrics, and most can even sing the first verse. But they don't understand the event they are singing about. Rockets' red glare? Bombs bursting in air? Was there a battle somewhere?

Yes. The Battle of Baltimore was one battle in the War of 1812 fought between the United States and Great Britain, one of the obscure squares in the quilt of American history. Few Americans know anything about this war, sometimes called the Second War for Independence.

I finally concluded that the national anthem and its connection to the Battle of Baltimore was the personal hook I would use to draw people into an activity. Yet the more I read about the Battle of Baltimore, the more I realized stories other than Key's were every bit as intriguing. I learned about the flag's seamstress, Mary Pickersgill, and the story of the man who devised the defense strategy for Baltimore. And those stories raised further questions. What about the British perspective? Who was behind the plan of attack? And why Baltimore? The British had just attacked Washington DC several days before. They had burned the Capitol and the White House. Why were they interested in Baltimore?

In the end I settled on telling the stories of five fascinating people. These multiple perspectives, woven together, created a richly compelling narrative.

Map Obsession

Besides introducing visitors to real people from history, another goal of the HOHR was letting visitors manipulate reproductions of historical sources and see the kinds of evidence from which historians draw interpretations of the past. By doing this rudimentary detective work, visitors could gain an understanding of the process of history. They could begin to answer the question: how do we know what we know? I always attempt to expose people to a variety of sources so they can learn the kinds of evidence that historians study. In the process they may also consider the evidence that they themselves are leaving for future historians to study.

A historian needs to know how to conduct research and must be skillful at linking historical sources. Because one source leads to another and another, often the story one is following takes a turn because a new source is uncovered. My work on the flag project put me on the trail of fascinating sources on both sides of the Atlantic Ocean. It took me to the major repositories of American history, such as the National Archives and the Library of Congress, and of British history, including Britain's Public Record Office. As the story unfolded, I was reminded again of how much I enjoyed the research process. Yet I still had not found a compelling source that could serve as the focal point of the activity.

One historical source I particularly like is maps. I have learned over the years that I'm not alone. Many people love maps, any kind of map—call us map geeks if you like. One day I read about a large military map of Baltimore drawn just before the Battle of Baltimore in 1814, now residing in the collection of the National Archives. I drove out to examine it at the Archives II building in College Park, Maryland, and was instantly enamored with the faded piece of paper. The large three-by-six-foot map was hand-drawn and colored with watercolors by an American military map maker named James Kearney. Kearney created it at the orders of Brigadier General Winder and it was titled "Sketch of the Military Topography of Baltimore and its vicinity and of Patapsco Neck to North Point." As I examined the map, my excitement mounted. Drawn for defensive purposes prior to the British attack on Baltimore, the map's scope showed Fort McHenry, North Point, Fells Point, and other important places associated with the story I wanted to tell. Since the HOHR did not have a map-based activity, this was just the find I needed—my main source.

The Characters in the Story

The Star-Spangled Banner story begins with Mary Pickersgill, who was born in Philadelphia in 1776. Her mother, Rebecca Young, a well-known flag maker, made blankets, uniforms, and flags for George Washington's Continental army. Mary learned her mother's trade. Given the small community of flag makers, we can assume Rebecca and Mary probably knew Betsy Ross. Later, when Mary's husband died unexpectedly, she decided to move with her daughter and mother to Baltimore, where her sister and brother-in-law, a sea captain, lived. Flag making was a flourishing craft in Baltimore due to flags and ship's colors needed for military and maritime industries. Mary settled into a small two-story house at 60 Albemarle Street in the Old Town neighborhood and opened a business.

In early summer of 1813, Maj. George Armistead, the new commander of Baltimore's Fort McHenry, sent one of his staff to place an order with Mary. He ordered two flags for the fort, a storm flag and a garrison flag. The smaller storm flag would be flown in bad weather. The garrison flag, thirty by forty-two feet and about one-quarter the size of a basketball court, was standard size for a fort and would be flown in fair weather. Its size guaranteed that people could see it from great distances. However, the textile was too large for Mary's small house. She and her thirteen-year-old daughter and a few other seamstresses took it to a nearby brewery, where they could spread it on the floor and work. The flags were delivered to Fort McHenry in August. At the end of October Mary received $168.54 for the storm flag and $405.90 for the garrison flag, which we now call the Star-Spangled Banner. Today the organization that runs the restored Pickersgill home as a museum owns the original receipt.

In 1814, Baltimore was the third largest city in the United States, with a population just over forty-five thousand. A bustling center of maritime enterprise, its ships sailed to ports around the world. While this in itself made the city a compelling target for the British, I quickly learned there was an even greater reason why the British would attack Baltimore. Fells Point shipyards were the center for the privateering business—government-sanctioned capture of British merchant ships. Goods from the captured ships were sold at auction and the privateer owners received a large share of the profits. Baltimore privateers had captured or sunk nearly five hundred British ships since the start of the war.

During the years leading up to the September 1814 battle, Thomas Kemp was building a shipping empire from the docks at Fells Point. He owned one of the largest shipyards in Baltimore, located at Washington and Alisanna Streets. During the War of 1812, Kemp's ships became famous for their speed and durability against British shipping. His shipyard built four of the most famous privateers, including the distinguished *Chasseur*, the pride of Baltimore. I read yellowed copies of the nineteenth-century *Niles' Weekly Register*, which compiled a monthly list of the "American Prizes," those British vessels captured by privateers. Thomas Kemp's ships were usually part of the action.

It is not surprising that Britain saw the situation through a diametrically opposed perspective. In 1813 the *London Star* wrote, "The American navy must be annihilated; her arsenals and dock yards must be consumed; and the turbulent inhabitants of Baltimore must be tamed with the weapons which shook the wooden turrets of Copenhagen." (In 1807, while at war with France, the British navy had destroyed the Danish fleet in Copenhagen harbor to keep it from falling into French hands.) In 1814 a different British paper wrote, "There is not a spot in the whole United States where an infliction of Britain's vengeance will be more entitled to our applause than on this sink of jacobinical infamy—Baltimore."

There clearly was motive for attack. But was there opportunity? With the American navy virtually nonexistent in the Chesapeake and the local militias in disarray, the British must have felt that they could do as they pleased. On August 24 the British army attacked Washington and burned the Capitol and the White House. As the British navy, under Scottish-born Vice Admiral Sir Alexander Cochrane, sailed up the Chesapeake Bay, its leaders decided on Baltimore as the next target and formed a plan of attack. Cochrane, as commander of the North American station, directed operations along the East Coast from his eighty-gun flagship, the HMS *Tonnant*. He apparently had been eager to destroy Washington and boasted that "Mr. Madison will be hurled from his throne."

Vice Admiral Cochrane and Major General Ross decided on a two-pronged attack—with the army attacking by land and the navy by sea. In July Cochrane had received a secret letter from Rear Admiral Cockburn, who cautioned that Baltimore's harbor was well protected by Fort McHenry and that shallow waters on the Patapsco River would not allow close access for large ships. He recommended a land attack. The British forces had overwhelmed the militias protecting Washington, and there was no reason to think Baltimore would be any different. I wanted to know if the secret letter still existed. Its contents were documented in a history book I'd read, but where was the letter? I set my intern, Emily, on the trail. Using her investigative skills, she found the letter in the collection of the National Library of Scotland.

The citizens of Baltimore knew their city was a prime target and, with the powerful British navy sailing up the Chesapeake Bay toward them, they anticipated an attack. The Committee of Vigilance and Safety chose Maj. Gen. Samuel Smith, a Revolutionary War veteran, to take command of Baltimore's defenses. Smith knew the British could attack by land or sea or both. One road led into the city from the east, and the likely place for the ships to unload was North Point, fourteen miles away at road's end. If the navy attacked, the city's prime defense was the star-shaped Fort McHenry, completed fourteen years earlier. While the troops at the fort under Major Armistead readied themselves for battle, Smith wanted to ensure that ships could not get into the harbor, even if they somehow made it past the fort. He devised a brilliant plan to completely block the harbor by authorizing troops to seize privately owned ships and sink them in the channels around the fort. Then he ordered nine barges constructed to guard the channel. A copy of his detailed plan still exists, along with various claims for reimbursement from the government from the owners of those confiscated ships.

As the British attack commenced on September 13, 1814, American Francis Scott Key found himself with a front-row seat behind enemy lines. A Georgetown lawyer, Key had been hired to facilitate the release of a friend captured by the British during the attack on Washington. This required getting the American government's permission to visit British leadership, meeting with the U.S. government's prisoner-exchange agent John Skinner, and finding the British fleet somewhere on the Chesapeake. Before he left, Key penned a quick note to his mother explaining the mission and sending his family to stay with her in Frederick. The party set out on a packet boat, under a flag of truce. Surprisingly, Key and Skinner quickly located the British fleet and during the exchange proceedings enjoyed the hospitality of the British officers, including Cochrane. When at last they finalized the release and prepared to go on their way, the British detained them because they had undoubtedly overheard plans for the attack. Skinner had raised the possibility of release with Vice Admiral Cochrane, who had replied: "Ah, Mr. Skinner, after discussing so freely our preparation and plans, you could hardly expect us to let you go on shore in advance of us." The British promised to release the Americans when the attack was over. Since there was no room on his flagship, Cochrane made arrangements for them to move to a frigate commanded by his son, Sir Thomas Cochrane. They were politely held captive until the military operation was completed.

Key was forced to watch the naval battle unfold from a boat about eight miles downriver from Fort McHenry. He could see flat barges holding mortars to fire the bombs silently move into position closer to the fort. Suddenly the attack began, and bomb blasts and whistling Congreve rockets filled the sky. The rockets' red glare came from the HMS *Erebus*, specially modified for launching rockets and called a rocket ship. My sources revealed that the logbook for the *Erebus* existed in the Public Record Office in England. I remember the thrill of opening the copied pages they sent. There, written in scratchy but neat handwriting, a crewman had written, "Tuesday, Sept. 13th, 1814, at 5:45 weighed [anchor] and made sail for off the enemy's fort . . . at 7 observed the bombs commence bombarding the Fort, fired Rockets at the Fort." The *Erebus*'s logbook tells its story in exacting detail.

I have to wonder if Key slept at all as the bombardment continued through the night. In the early hours of the morning, "dawn's early light," the British guns ceased firing. Key eagerly peered through a telescope and saw Mary Pickersgill's American flag flying over the fort above the lingering smoke of battle. The Americans had been victorious. Inspired by the sight, he began to jot down lyrics for a song, the song that years later became America's national anthem. Twenty years after this event, he wrote about the moment of inspiration. "The song, I know, came from the heart . . . in that hour of deliverance and joyful triumph, my heart spoke; and 'Does not such a country, and such defenders of their country, deserve a song?' was its question. With it came an inspiration not to be resisted."

Key's song was first published as the "Defence of Fort McHenry" in a broadside on September 17, several days after the battle. The publication indicated it should be sung to a popular British tune, "Anacreon in Heaven." This tune was not a drinking song as is often stated but the club song of an eighteenth-century gentlemen's musical club, the Anacreontic Society. Key most likely knew the tune. Soon newspapers up and down the East Coast printed the song and the Star-Spangled Banner grew in popularity, until it became the official national anthem of the United States in 1931.

Digging for Sources

In the end I accomplished what I set out to do. I told a little-known story through focus on the map. I hired an artist to improve the legibility of the Winder map, enhancing the colors, cleaning it up, and making the key locations easier to find. Visitors followed the story by finding locations on the map and marking them with magnets. Testing of the activity revealed that other than map geeks, few visitors had the patience to spend much time looking for points on the map. We ended up providing hints to guide them toward quadrants of the map. Other historical sources provided additional clues.

Researching this story proved to be one of the most interesting projects of my career. The activity ended up including reproductions of more than ten primary sources that together told the story. The collections of the National Archives offered the Winder map and a master carpenter's certificate signed by Thomas Kemp. The Flag House Museum held the flag receipt. The Maryland Historical Society contributed an 1816 Baltimore City Directory listing the Pickersgill business and a watercolor by an unidentified artist depicting the view from the harbor looking past the fort and showing the nine barges. I found the handwritten document detailing Smith's plan at the Library of Congress, along with a British midshipman's account of the naval battle published in 1841. The National Library of Scotland yielded the secret letter sent to Cochrane, and the Public Record Office of the United Kingdom held the HMS *Erebus* rocket ship logbook. And, the archives of the National Museum of American History held a copy of the *Nile's Weekly Register* that contained news reports about the British opinion of Baltimore.

I found portraits of everyone but Thomas Kemp. A copy of Cochrane's portrait came from the National Portrait Gallery of Scotland. To top it all off, I was able to include bomb fragments of the correct artillery type and an original Congreve rocket from the museum's collections. It was not on display and I was thrilled when the curators agreed that it should be part of my activity, hanging out of reach of hands. I also found some impressive and heavy bomb fragments to put on display. Since they were almost indestructible, visitors could touch them and try to imagine an entire bomb flying in their direction. By telling the story through these primary sources, I hoped to help visitors see the hard evidence that historians base their interpretations on and gain an appreciation for the many perspectives surrounding one story.

My research also included trips to Baltimore. While the look and size of the city have changed dramatically from the Winder map depiction, Baltimore's historical essence remains in its fascinating small neighborhoods and lively, rejuvenated harbor area. The cobblestoned streets of Fells Point remain popular with Baltimore residents and visitors alike. Though the shipbuilding industries have long since disappeared, the historic stone buildings house great seafood restaurants and lively bars. The staff at Mary Pickersgill's restored home welcomes students and visitors from all over the country. Tour guides like to point out that the flag was so large Mary was forced to complete it on the floor of the nearby brewery. The North Point landing site is located at Fort Howard. Much of the peninsula today is part of North Point State Park, a recreational area layered with history. In the early 1900s it was the location of the popular Bay Shore Amusement Park. Today the old pier, a restored fountain, and a trolley station are all that remain. The road from North Point winds through a variety of landscapes, including fields and both industrial and residential areas. Monuments along the way memorialize the actions of the various skirmishes that halted the British land attack.

No visit to Baltimore is complete without a trip to the well-preserved Fort McHenry, a property owned and interpreted by the National Park Service. The thick brick walls of the fort serve as a reminder of that ferocious bombardment and on calm days, a visitor might see a huge flag on the fort's flagpole. The view of the shimmering Patapsco River from the artillery posts at the corners of the fort is spectacular on a sunny day. One can just imagine the incoming bombs. The rockets, new technology of the day, proved inaccurate and rarely hit a target. But the bombs fell for hours at the rate of one per minute. No matter what time of day or year a person visits, it is not difficult to imagine the moment described by British midshipman Robert Barrett, a witness to the bombardment: "As the last vessel spread her canvas to the wind, the Americans hoisted a splendid and superb ensign on their battery, and at the same time fired a gun of defiance."

Today visitors to the National Museum of American History can view the Star-Spangled Banner on permanent display in a new state-of-the-art exhibition space. Oh, say, does that Star-Spangled Banner yet wave? Well, no, not really. It appears to float in space, resting on a large angled table in dim light. While its fragility remains obvious, its powerful symbolism continues to stir patriotic hearts. And a portrait of Mary Pickersgill hangs near her creation.

8
THAT STRANGE CREATURE THE MULE

My favorite animal is the mule. He has more
horse sense than a horse. He knows when to stop
eating—and he knows when to stop working.

—*President Harry S. Truman, son of a mule dealer*

Historical threads firmly tie present to the past. Historical traditions find myriad ways to flourish in our modern world. History can also intersect with one's present in the most unexpected ways. I never imagined that a job in Washington DC would lead me to a deeper understanding of the culture of my rural Pennsylvania childhood. But in teaching museum visitors historical American agricultural practices, I uncovered evidence of my own family's rich agricultural history.

One activity in the Hands On History Room centered on a life-size fiberglass model of a mule. Dubbed "Jefferson" by Chelsea Clinton on one of her childhood visits to the museum, the mule stood patiently while visitors tried to harness him. By carefully following the directions, anyone could reach success. Without the directions, however, the harness could become hopelessly tangled. Entire families became engaged in the process. I thought it great fun to stand and watch while a determined father would encourage his kids to help him harness the mule. Many a man, following the modus operandi of his gender, would presume to know how to harness a mule and would not pay attention to the guide sheet. Inevitably the harness would get twisted and the kids would lose interest and wander off to another activity. A resolute father would try to untangle the mess while a hopelessly frustrated father would walk away and leave it to the staff's expertise. The successful family that either followed the directions or had been fortunate enough to own horses finished with pride. Staff were usually around to coach or help visitors and took numerous photos of families posing by the harnessed mule. Our goal was casual conversation with visitors about the role of mules in American history, hoping to foster a new appreciation for farmers of the past.

Mules are strange animals. The offspring of a female horse and a male donkey, a mule cannot reproduce because it does not have the correct number of chromosomes. A mule exhibits the long ears of its father and the strength and agility of its mother. While the animal is generally known for its stubborn attitude, a mule is quite smart. It knows when to stop and wait. I've been told that if a mule gets caught in barbed wire, it won't thrash about and injure itself, but will stop and wait patiently for someone to rescue it. And a mule knows how to listen to its body, knowing when to stop working, eating, or drinking. Apparently a horse can work, eat, or drink itself to death.

George Washington, Mule Lover

One person who strongly advocated for the use of mules was America's first president. Besides his role as founding father, George Washington was an avid mule breeder and receives much credit for introducing mules to American agriculture and promoting their use throughout the South. In the 1700s the Spanish were using mules in various capacities and had sent mules to their missions in western

North America. Not long after the Revolutionary War, Washington, an ardent farmer, decided to experiment with mules. He set out to import a donkey from Spain, but the country restricted exports. The King of Spain somehow heard of Washington's wish and came to the rescue. He packed up two donkeys and shipped them to America. Only one survived the trip and ended up in Boston by mistake. Washington sent for the donkey with directions to his staff to treat the animal with great care. The huge donkey, whom he named Royal Gift, finally arrived at Washington's estate, Mount Vernon, and stood over fifteen hands high (that's about five feet just to the top of the withers). At first Royal Gift did not show any romantic interest in Washington's stable of horses. Washington wrote William Fitzhugh about the problem: "I have my hopes, that when he [Royal Gift] becomes a little better acquainted with Republican enjoyments, he will amend his manners and fall into our custom of doing business." Eventually he decided that the Virginia mares weren't so bad and Mount Vernon witnessed the birth of a mule.

In 1786 the French general the Marquis de Lafayette heard about his American friend's interest in mules and surprised Washington by sending him a male donkey, who arrived at the port of Baltimore from the Island of Malta. Named the Knight of Malta, the donkey did his job and increased Mount Vernon's mule population. Livestock inventories at Mount Vernon show a swift shift from horses to mules during the years that Washington was President. In 1785 the inventory listed 130 horses and no mules, and by 1799 it listed 58 mules and 25 horses.

Washington quickly became convinced that mules would transform American agriculture. In comparison to horses, mules endured heat better, required less quality feed, fought less in large groups, and were generally healthier. He wrote to Arthur Young in 1788, "I have a prospect of introducing into this country a very excellent race of animals . . . from these I hope to secure a race of extraordinary goodness, which will stock the country." And he wasted no time in his efforts. Farmer Washington sent poor (or lucky) Royal Gift on a stud tour throughout the South, displaying him at agricultural shows and happily accepting breeding requests. Washington even encouraged his friend Thomas Jefferson to try mules, and Jefferson came to favor them.

Today, the staff at the restored Mount Vernon interpret Washington's roles not only as general and first president, but as farmer. Shortly after the Hands On History Room opened, the Mount Vernon staff decided to develop a hands-on history tent for their visitors. They consulted with my colleagues and ended up with their own fiberglass version of the HOHR mule Jefferson. Painted a reddish color, it saw years of use and abuse at the hands of eager visitors attempting to harness it. But Mount Vernon was able to go a step farther. Since it includes a working farm site with animals, Mount Vernon is able to show visitors the real thing. I decided to visit the estate's two mules.

When I arrived, Lisa Pregent, the livestock manager, was busy trying to coax two escaped oxen back to their fenced pasture. The oxen shared a pasture with eight or so large horses and Moose, one very large Mammoth donkey. Lisa took me to the adjacent field and introduced me to James and Clem (also called Kate and Kit behind the scenes). Kentucky-born, the mules take visitors for wagon rides and help with the plowing and harrowing at the farm site. They endure hours of continuous petting from visitors and only go out in public every couple days. On their days off they graze on succulent grasses under the azure Virginia sky. Such is the life of a Mount Vernon mule charged with helping to tell the story of George Washington's fascination with mules to a million visitors each year.

Amish Riddle

I have seen many mules in my lifetime. Having grown up in Amish Country in Lancaster County, Pennsylvania, I knew that Amish farmers today still work with mules. The Amish, a religious sect whose members have settlements in various states, are well known for driving horse-drawn carriages called buggies, dressing in plain clothes, avoiding worldly temptations, and living simply. The Lancaster settlement maintains the second largest population in the United States and hundreds of tidy Amish farms dot the countryside. Amish farmers do not use tractors—they use mules or draft horses to pull their agricultural equipment. The Amish community in Lancaster is especially fond of mules and uses them for much of the fieldwork. Any tourist driving the rolling country roads of Lancaster, unless there in the dead of winter, will see Amish mule teams at work in the fields.

The context of the activity in the Hands On History Room explained the role of mules in history, but I decided that it was important to show visitors a connection to the use of mules today. Mules plod the trails in the Grand Canyon, carrying visitors and supplies into the canyon. Their surefootedness makes them ideal for this job. Until the invention of helicopters, the military used mules around the world to gain access to remote, rugged areas. Mules at several historic canal sites, such as the C&O canal at Great Falls near Washington and the National Canal Museum in Pennsylvania, pull visitors in reconstructed barges. Yet agriculture, not transportation, was the interpretive focus of the HOHR activity.

The Amish provided the obvious link, so why not create a book of photographs? One problem with this idea: the Amish religion disallows any sort of portrait photography because it promotes individualism at the expense of community and can lead to pride. I contacted a photographer from a Lancaster newspaper who agreed to help. He sent me a wonderful collection of his photographs of Amish farmers and their mules, all shot with a clear sensitivity to the photography taboo.

My supporting research revealed some fascinating information. The obvious first question most people have is: why use mules and not tractors? The reason encapsulates the challenge that outsiders often have trying to understand Amish culture and has a basis in both religion and society. The existence of tractors has lured young Amish farmers from the very beginning of the invention. According to scholar Donald Kraybill, the Amish began using tractors in the 1920s, when they first appeared. However, Amish leaders banned their use in about 1923, seeing the tractor as a threat to several foundational principles of Amish society: community and work. The Amish want to preserve their community and way of life and recognize as a threat anything that encourages members to create distance from the community. Kraybill writes that the Amish leadership had already allowed the use of a variety of new farm equipment, but some leaders questioned whether the tractor was going too far. They viewed the car, which allowed easy travel at great distances, as a major threat to community—was a tractor dangerously close to a car? According to Kraybill, "Tractors did not have rubber tires yet, but they were self-propelled, autonomous, independently mobile—suspiciously similar to a car." From the 1930s through the early 1960s new and improved tractor models continued to tempt young Amish farmers.

The ban on tractors remains today and Kraybill says the most cited reason is the fear that they will lead to cars. In his book *The Riddle of Amish Culture*, Kraybill offers some examples of progressive Amish who permitted tractors in the field. They put rubber tires on the tractors and started riding them into town, and the line between tractor and car quickly blurred. Kraybill poses the interesting question of whether the Amish might be using tractors today if they had been invented before the car. Perhaps.

But among the other compelling reasons for not using tractors is the fact that they save labor—and the Amish welcome work as the "heartbeat of their community." Ultimately Amish leaders want to perpetuate a horse subculture. New generations learn about the care and feeding of mules and horses, and harness makers and blacksmiths maintain a thriving business. From a practical perspective, horses and mules are easier to handle in the field, do not pack the soil, and are cheaper.

To ensure that the new photo book would be engaging, I first tested the concept with museum visitors. I learned that most people didn't realize that Amish farmers used mules. They found the photos compelling. After initial audience testing, the final hurdle involved ensuring the accompanying text was accurate. The usual way to do this is to show a prototype to a content expert and in this case, that expert was an Amishman. But finding one who would talk to me was no easy task.

While I grew up near Amish people, in a suburb surrounded by Amish farms, I didn't know any Amish, since they generally keep to themselves. I considered my interactions with Amish over the years and thought back to my bus trips to school. The bus stopped to pick up an Amish boy about my age at a nearby farm and dropped him off at the one-room schoolhouse en route to the high school. How many school bus rides in this country make a stop at a one-room school? He sat by himself in the front of the bus and no one ever talked to him. At the time it seemed quite natural to pick up an Amish boy on the way to school, but I've since understood the rarity. I wish now that I had befriended him. Looking back I realize that I missed a rare opportunity to gain access into another culture by not reaching out.

The museum's mule harness had been crafted by Amish harness makers in Intercourse, Pennsylvania, and museum staff had shipped the fiberglass mule up to Pennsylvania for an exact fit. One can only imagine the talk in the Amish community when a truck from the Smithsonian appeared bearing Jefferson. On occasion, when the harness needed repair, I made a trip home and drove over to Intercourse. The harness maker's shop sat on a side street of the village, not far from the post office that is a photo stop on every tourist's itinerary. The shop received few non-Amish customers due to the hand-printed sign on the door: "No tourists." It was a small pleasant shop with wood flooring. Upon entering a powerful mixture of kerosene and leather hit my nose. The light fixtures hanging above were kerosene lamps, since the Amish do not connect to the electrical grid. The neatly organized shelves overflowed with fascinating products related to horse culture, and the narrow aisles made navigation a challenge. My trips to the shop felt like traveling back in time. A tall, thin Amish woman, in a simple hand-sewn dark purple dress with a black apron, always ran the register and greeted me cautiously. She wore a white mesh bonnet with straps hanging down, her hair tucked neatly under it. The Amish who ran the store were never talkative; there was a shyness about them, an awkwardness. This sometimes came across as aloofness, but I concluded that it was simply their way. They were never unfriendly, just people of few words. The shop employees were, not farmers, so I decided they were not the best people to ask about mules.

Tracking Down an Expert

One day during my search for an Amish farmer, I learned that my parents' neighbors across the street were friends with an Amish family. My dad had met them and the father seemed an ideal candidate to be my "expert." One can't telephone an Amishman to schedule an appointment. Phones are generally forbidden in Amish homes. The neighbor told the man that I wanted to stop by. My dad and I drove out to the farm, several minutes from my parents' house. Just past a white one-room schoolhouse, we turned left and drove up the dusty lane, parking between the brick farmhouse and barn. It was a late spring day and the doors were wide open, the cheery chatter of kids in the air. I was a little nervous, not having made a definite appointment. Jacob's wife came to the door wiping her hands on her apron. She pointed to Jacob in the field, plowing—with his mules! What could have been more perfect . . . the expert with his mules.

We walked out to him, and he stopped the team. I introduced myself, careful to mention that he knew my parents' neighbor. I explained my business and how I hoped he could help me. I did not even know if he would recognize the Smithsonian name. He agreed right there on the spot to read my text, and after a quick read-through, pronounced it accurate. It was a surreal moment, like many in my career, where I couldn't believe I was standing there in a freshly plowed field as an Amishman read my work. His young face, bronzed by the sun, sported an untrimmed beard about seven inches long. A dirty wide-brimmed straw hat kept the sun from his eyes. I guessed we were close in age, but what different worlds we inhabited. We probably grew up less than two miles from each other, yet our lives were vastly dissimilar. What would my life have been like had I been born into his world?

Weeks later I mailed Jacob a letter on Smithsonian stationery thanking him for his help. I invited him to journey to Washington to see the mule. He never came. Other Amish people did, however. I was always happy to see the Amish at the Smithsonian. They paid "Englishmen" (their term for non-Amish) to drive them or took the train. In their distinctive dress they stand out in a crowd and it is fun to watch other people reacting to them. I often wondered what went through their minds as they looked at the collection of first ladies' gowns or Archie Bunker's chair. What did they think when they looked at the Hall of Transportation with its collection of carriages and cars from the past? What did American history mean to them? Did they care about America's past or were the nation's treasures just objects of curiosity? Do they see themselves as part of American culture?

The Mule Auction

I continued to see Jacob and his family on occasion and welcomed the opportunity to visit their farm. They once mentioned a mule auction that takes place three times each year during the late winter months. One year, seeking a new cultural experience, I decided to go. Mel's Stables sits on a windy country road outside of New Holland, Pennsylvania. My dad and I pulled up at the farm complex on an early spring day and knew we were in the right place—dozens of buggies were parked in an adjacent field and Amishmen stood in small groups scattered around the property. Through the windows, we could see a wall of straw hats.

We parked and entered the barn . . . mules were everywhere, more mules than I'd ever seen in my life. Stall after stall was filled with mules of many different colors and sizes. We walked over to the showing area, a sixty-by-ten-foot track, bleachers on one side and standing room and an auctioneer's table on the other. The auctioneer, presumably Mel, was already into his stuttering cadence. We stopped in our tracks, entranced by the spectacle around us. We had walked into a totally different culture—surrounded by a sea of straw hats, black coats, and beards, we were a minority. It was yet another time travel moment, for the time could have been the mid-nineteenth century.

The audience intently watched the action taking place in the showing area. An Amish handler would run a single mule or team, stopping and starting to demonstrate the animals' reflexes and agility. About four young men had the job of leading the mules. They lined up like circus performers waiting for a turn in the spotlight, then ran the mule one way and then the other. Once a boy got on top of a pair of mules and stood up straddling them, trying to show off the mules' ability to work as a team. He lost his balance and fell off, those nearby running to make sure he was okay. Sometimes the handler halted a team and directed it to back up—slowly as a team, impressing the crowd.

We asked a young father standing nearby where the mules came from. All over the United States, was the answer—Kentucky, Alabama, Michigan. He told us that a mule can work for ten to twenty years before it is too old. He also explained that the males are called jacks and the females are mollys.

We stood in a small group of about twelve Amishmen at the end of the showing track. One particular mule, high-strung, young, and not broken, decided he did not want to play this game. He yanked his tether from the guy holding it and started running directly at us. The crowd scattered, looking for any place away from the kicking animal. He then turned suddenly and ran in the other direction, stopped, turned, and ran toward us again. In that moment I was scared that I would be maimed at a mule auction. Yet it was funny to see so many men in black scatter to any available corner. After several minutes, the mule's handler regained control and order was restored.

The official auction list described 245 mules for sale. We quickly learned the variables that affected price: age, size, work experience, and skills. Each mule was labeled: broke, not broke, green broke, Amish broke, southern broke, jockey stick broke, halter broke, or line broke. Buyers had an array of colors to choose from: black, sorrel, white, blond, bay, red sorrel; and according to the program, several different energy levels were represented, including "works with snap," "a fast walker," and "gets a little slow at the end of the day." An owner described his seven-year-old sorrel jack mule this way: "I wanted him for a riding mule but he has too much smoke for that!"

I also learned that "smooth mouth" meant the mule was older than ten and his age was hard to tell.

We moved to the bleachers and settled in near the auction official watching our section of the crowd. With a crisp, high-pitched "Ho," he communicated with the auctioneer that the bid was met and the caller knew to up the price. I watched him scan the crowd. What was the bidder's sign, I wondered. I looked for a wave of the hand, a printed number, anything. Until I deciphered the code, I was scared to let my eyes meet the official's gaze for fear I'd end up going home with a mule. I thought I detected a slight nod. "Ho!" The price went up. Was it a nod or a wink? I didn't want to admit my ignorance and never did learn the bidders' code. I could have asked the older man sitting next to me. He was actively following the action and at one point asked me the winning price of the last sale. $3,250 was the highest price I heard that day; $75 was the bargain. The bargain mules were the elderly ones and the young ones that needed a lot of attention and training.

I observed the people around me. Some older men with white beards. Some single men with no beards. (Untrimmed beards are required at marriage and serve as a sort of wedding ring. Mustaches are forbidden by the church, supposedly because hair above the lips was once associated with military officers, who persecuted the Amish in their past.) Some young men in their twenties had small children in tow. The children dressed as miniatures of their parents. All of them wore a hat, since the Amish code says a hat should be worn whenever outside the house. Around the age of two Amish boys start wearing hats. Each man seemed to have huge hands—I wondered if it was the developed muscles of everyday use or a genetic disposition evolved from generations of farmers. Some smoked cigars, some munched on chicken legs.

In a peanut gallery of sorts overlooking the far end of the auction area sat the women in their prayer caps. A large picture window allowed them to view the action and talk to their heart's content. At lunchtime they disappeared to help with the food. A food stand on the upper level featured many of the staples of a good Pennsylvania

Dutch diet, including chicken corn soup, slices of shoo-fly pie (made with molasses), raisin pies, vanilla pies, whoopie pies (a type of jumbo sandwich cookie—four-inch circular chocolate cakes with creamy white icing in the middle), and soft pretzels.

With the staccato calling of the auctioneer, the running mules, and the occasional chicken or pigeon flying recklessly through the showing area, it was a feast for the senses. Not to mention the smells . . . a cauldron of smells that should not mix—tobacco, manure, "barn," and good food.

Finally it was time to go. The auction would continue for about four more hours, but we had work to do. As we walked to our car, we observed two young Amishmen trying to load a pair of mules into a red trailer. One mule refused to move. The men were straining and pulling, trying to force the animal to step up into the dark space. Apparently the mule had decided that he had suffered enough indignity for a day and didn't want to take a risky step toward an unknown future. I overheard one of his handlers mutter, "Stubborn as a mule."

A Personal Connection

Farmers have used mules during most of our nation's history. George Washington's vision for American agriculture blossomed, and by the 1920s the mule population in the United States reached five million, which represented half of the world's mule population. The invention of motor-powered tractors did not signal the instant end of mule-powered agriculture. In 1906 International Harvester debuted a single cylinder tractor, but it wasn't until the mid-1920s that a general, all-purpose tractor entered the market. These tractors, however, were large clunky contraptions that didn't suit the smaller farms in places like Pennsylvania.

Many non-Amish Lancaster farmers continued working with mules, including my grandfather, J. Martin Esbenshade. Grandpa was a tobacco farmer for much of his life. He died when I was three but left a record of his farming days in journals he kept from the 1920s through the 1960s. The entries document daily activities and weather. From the journals I learned that he had owned and used mules into the 1940s. I immediately asked my mother and my aunt about the mules, Pete and Pet, and found out that their grandfather had also owned mules. I had not realized that mules were a part of my heritage.

One day during a weekend visit to Lancaster I was sifting through items once owned by my grandparents and happened upon a large photograph of two mule teams standing in front of plows in a field. A sturdy-looking farmer sat in the seat of each plow, one with a big mustache, looking a lot like Tom Selleck. Next to one of the plows stood four boys lined up in a row from tallest to smallest. My aunt identified them as my grandfather and his brothers—my grandfather was the tallest brother. We estimated the photograph's date was 1913.

In the Hands On History Room, the mule activity connected to an exhibition in the museum about the African American migration from rural South to urban North. The photographs surrounding the activity showed Southern black farmers working with mules. I thought we should include historical images that represented other regions of the country. The photo of my grandfather and great-grandfather showed a Northern family in the same time period. I decided to en-large the photo and hang it by Jefferson. While the photo was used for illustration purposes only and never became part of the Smithsonian collection, I was proud that for a few years at least, a photo of my grandfather was hanging in the Smithsonian. As a result of Jefferson, the fiberglass mule, I learned a piece of my family heritage.

9
WHEN HOUSES TALK

Houses are like the human beings that inhabit them.

—*Victor Hugo*

I am not a person who frequents open houses on Sundays and I rarely go on spring garden and holiday home tours. But when visiting a city with an interesting past, it doesn't take me long to track down the historic district and walk its streets and peer into its buildings. My favorite place to house gawk is Charleston, South Carolina. Its historic area south of Broad Street has no rivals. I love to stroll its streets at night and gaze into brightly lit rooms that reveal gleaming antiques and old paintings. Other historic districts on my top-ten list include Philadelphia's Society Hill, Boston's Beacon Hill, and Old Town Alexandria and Richmond's Fan district in Virginia. The gawking is easiest in those old East Coast cities where the houses sit close to the narrow streets. It proves harder in the Midwest and the West, where houses sit farther from the sidewalks. There is no shame in house gawking. A friend who lived in the Fan district once told me that the homeowners there take pride in keeping the curtains open for all to see their excellent taste. Historic houses, whether museums or private, hold an allure precisely because they are homes with the potential to tell the stories of their people.

One of my favorite projects while at the National Museum of American History focused on the largest artifact in the museum's collection. It is not the steam locomotive Southern Railway No. 1401 or the revolutionary-era gunboat *Philadelphia*, the oldest preserved warship in America. The largest artifact is an almost 250-year-old house that stood at 16 Elm Street in Ipswich, Massachusetts, thirty miles north of Boston. In 1963 the town planned to raze the house and build a parking lot, but several earnest members of the local historical society came up with a plan to save the house the very day the backhoe arrived to tear it down. They paid the crew chief to wait until they called the Smithsonian.

There are various reasons why a Smithsonian curator might not accept a donation of an artifact. Lack of storage space is one of them. One would think that the Smithsonian might not have space to store a house, but the staff at the American History Museum, then known as the Museum of History and Technology, decided to accept the gift. They were trying to fill the new museum, which opened in 1964. The house was carefully documented, dismantled, and shipped to Washington, where in 1966 it was reassembled. The staff members who collected the house put it on display as a representative example of early American building practices. The exhibition remained on view for many years, and while the staff eventually suggested a reinterpretation, this didn't happen. Finally the museum built temporary walls around it to accommodate new exhibitions and essentially the house was put into storage. It became a secret artifact as visitors to the museum were not even aware of its existence. In the late 1990s, however, the house's period of slumber finally came to an end when new curators, funding in hand, embarked on a project to research the inhabitants of the house. The time had come to tear down the walls, put this huge artifact back on display and let it tell new stories.

A Peek at America's Homes

There are over eight thousand historic house museums in America, ranging from the small dark apartments of America's immigrants in the Lower East Side Tenement Museum in Manhattan to the estates of the fabulously rich and famous like the Vanderbilts' Biltmore Estate in North Carolina and Hearst Castle on the Pacific Coast. Some tell the story of their well-known inhabitants, others of their equally famous architects. Historic houses come in all shapes and sizes and varieties. Yes, some are even houses of ill repute. An interpretive tour of a historic brothel in Cripple Creek, Colorado, remains etched in my mind because it offered an unexpected look at a part of Western history that gets overlooked.

I've often wondered how so many house museums can manage to keep their doors open to visitors. My conclusion is that people are generally curious about how others lived. We live our private lives within the walls of our homes, and historic house museums offer a peek into the most personal spaces. They reveal our tastes, our priorities, and sometimes our secrets. If you want to learn about a person, visit his home. Few homes reflect their owner more than Monticello, Thomas Jefferson's retreat near Charlottesville, Virginia. Perched on a small mountain and surrounded by the foothills of the Blue Ridge, the house has been called Jefferson's autobiographical masterpiece. He designed the house, which is imbued with his personality and creativity. His many inventions are scattered throughout. In the entrance hall his great clock with its cannonball-size weights gongs the hours and indicates days of the week. Near his bookcases sits a cube-shaped revolving book stand with adjustable rests for holding books.

The homes of famous people hold an intrinsic power, an almost palpable nearness to history. At Susan B. Anthony's restored house in Rochester, New York, one of the staff members told me of a visitor who made such a strong emotional connection to the place that she burst into tears on the sidewalk in front of the house when her tour guide told her that Miss Anthony had walked on those same bricks. Nineteenth-century author Sarah Orne Jewett wrote about visiting the home of the Brontë sisters in England: "Nothing you ever read about them can make you know them until you go there. Never mind people who tell you there is nothing to see in the place where people lived who interest you. You always find something of what made them the souls they were. And at any rate, you see their sky and their earth." Frederick Douglass's home, Cedar Hill, commands a spectacular view over Washington DC. I remember standing in his library, sun streaming through the large windows. I imagined him sitting at the heavy wooden desk and looking for a book in the crammed bookcases. What powerful words flowed from his pen in that space.

Historians and other staff who serve as stewards of historic homes face the daunting challenge of deciding which stories a house should tell. Sometimes the stories might not reflect well on the property owner and might not be well received. Yet many historic homes of famous people teeter dangerously on the verge of "great-man history" interpretations. As historian John Herbst puts it: "[T]he beliefs of those who led the drive to preserve the house continue to shape the policy even after the house has been turned into a working museum." Visitors to historic homes must remember that the residents were complex individuals who faced trials and tribulations just like everyone, and the staff at these properties must be willing to talk about tough topics such as financial challenges and moral issues. Talking about the topic of slavery, for example, continues to challenge the staff at museum homes.

Like many millions of Americans I have made a pilgrimage to one of the most visited historic houses in the United States, George Washington's Mount Vernon, located several miles across and down the Potomac River from Washington DC. In a busy year a million visitors come to see where the first President ate, entertained, and slept. In different ways than Monticello, Mount Vernon attests to the interests and private life of a man every school student learns about. I once visited during Christmas and was amused to see a live camel on display near the house. The staff was recreating 1787, when George Washington paid eighteen shillings (not a small sum) to bring a camel to the estate to entertain his guests. The third floor where Mrs. Washington spent her final years after her husband's death is open to visitors a few times a year. Above it, up a steep ladder, is the cupola where Washington looked through his telescope at traffic on the river. In the basement, with its exposed beams and floorboards original to the earliest part of the house, visitors can see the cornerstone, carved with a prominent LW, for Lawrence Washington, Washington's older half-brother who first lived at the estate. The sprawling property includes the white mansion, outbuildings, a wharf, gardens, a sixteen-sided barn, and the relatively recent addition of a reconstructed slave cabin. Like Jefferson, Washington owned many slaves. And, as in Colonial Williamsburg, the staff has struggled to identify the best way to present the topic. Besides the slave cabin, the property features a monument to the enslaved people who lived on the property, and their descendants appear on video along with historians talking about their impressions of Washington and slavery.

Presidential homes offer profound insight into the character of their occupants, especially when preserved in the context of the community around them. My favorites include Lyndon Johnson's boyhood home—a small white frame house in the town of Johnson City, Texas, west of Austin. The simple house reveals his working class roots and its inhabitants' deep connection to the community. Harry Truman's home in Independence, Missouri, provides a glimpse into this man who retired to a modest house and walked the streets of the neighborhood daily. In Calvin Coolidge's family farmhouse in Plymouth Notch, Vermont, you can stand in the room where he took the oath of office from his father, the local notary public, to become president in 1923 upon the sudden death of Warren Harding. The homestead, tucked into the surrounding green mountains, was a fount of his deep country values. With a little imagination, visitors to Sagamore Hill, Teddy Roosevelt's sprawling Oyster Bay, New York, home can hear the excited shouts of children as they follow their father outside on another adventure. Exotic animal pelts on the floors and large verandas with views of the fields and water help a visitor to imagine a president whose soul was nourished by the natural world.

A collection of Franklin Roosevelt homes interprets the life of one of America's most influential families. The family estate in Hyde Park, New York, overlooks the Hudson River and hosted kings, queens, and prime ministers. A special wheelchair that FDR designed himself offers a powerful reminder of the obstacles he overcame. Several miles down the road sits Mrs. Roosevelt's Val-Kill Cottage. The small house was her office and retreat and is the only National Historic Site dedicated to a first lady. The bathroom's mirrors and shower head were mounted high on the walls because Mrs. Roosevelt was tired of stooping over. The Roosevelts' deep red summer cottage on Campobello Island, New Brunswick, is another spectacular place to peek behind the scenes into the family's life. A visitor can see the room where Roosevelt woke up one night with the paralysis that would profoundly change his life. The house sits surrounded by the meadows, lakes, and bays where the family spent many happy days. It is the only international historic site jointly owned and operated by Canada and the United States.

At a different point on the historic house spectrum sits Graceland, Elvis Presley's house in Tennessee. While not a fan of the iconic singer, I felt an obligation as a historian to visit the home during a trip to Memphis. The glimpse into his personal life with its 1970s fashion excesses proved captivating. The place screams its owner's personality and, like most houses, showcases his tastes and reveals his secrets. The jungle room's bright green shag carpet, carpeted ceiling, and waterfall illustrate the imaginative décor of the decade. An audio tour narrated by ex-wife Priscilla and daughter Lisa Marie

guides visitors through the house and provides a feeling of imme-
diacy, as if the King had just left.

One of My Favorite Homes

Not every historical house was owned or built by someone famous.
One of my favorite homes falls into this category. Drayton Hall,
an imposing eighteenth-century plantation house, stands in lofty
isolation amid moss-draped live oaks overlooking the Ashley River,
about nine miles northwest of Charleston, South Carolina. The
brick building, a survivor of earthquakes, hurricanes, poverty, and
two wars, is one of the few remaining vestiges of life before the
Civil War. At Drayton, the attraction is the house itself rather than
the family who built it and lived there.

This National Trust for Historic Preservation property is significant to historians and preservationists for its history, its rarity, its
condition, and its architectural style. It is the last surviving complete plantation house on the Ashley River, which in its heyday
was lined with many splendid houses of South Carolina's most
prominent families. In 1802 John Drayton explained the genesis of
these homes: "[G]entlemen of fortune were invited to form these
happy retreats from noise and bustle; the banks of the Ashley, as
being near the metropolis of the state was first the object of their
attention."

Drayton Hall has survived two and a half centuries in almost
its original condition. Built between 1738 and 1742, the house was
owned by seven generations of the Drayton family and was never
modernized with central heating, electricity, or plumbing. Its interior was repainted once. Historians consider the house one of the
finest and earliest examples of Georgian Palladian architecture in
America—the sophistication of its design was far ahead of any other
work being built in the American colonies at the time.

John Drayton built the house as his family's main residence, for
occupation in the winter season from mid-November to mid-May. It
was among the first products of a so-called rice prosperity. The suc-

cessful cultivation of vast plantations of cash crops brought sudden wealth to the men who may not have been members of the upper classes in the Old World. Family records leave the impression that Drayton Hall was the business and administrative center of the Drayton empire. Drayton wanted to express his position in society, and the ideal way to accomplish this was to copy the current styles in the mother country, England.

I first visited Drayton Hall the spring after Hurricane Hugo had blown through the previous fall. Before-and-after photographs showed the extent of the damage to hundreds of trees on the property. Even so, I found the starkness enthralling. Years later, on a cloudy March day, I visited again and was happy to see that nature was rebuilding and the holes from Hugo were filled with new growth. Once again I was transfixed by the isolation. The august house sits several hundred yards back from the river, and while the river side was considered the front (since guests arrived by boat), today visitors drive over from Charleston on highway 61, the Ashley River Road. Their first view is a two-story portico with Doric columns on the first floor and Ionic columns on the second.

Most visitors to historic homes expect to see a furnished house. Drayton, however, is completely empty. Its story focuses on the fine craftsmanship of its architectural details and its functionality over time. A grand staircase dominates the huge entrance hall and the rooms feature rich paneling, ornately carved plaster ceilings, and carved marble fireplace mantels. The stories of the occupants echo off the wooden floorboards and paneled walls. One family legend is a testament to the house's endurance. Civil War general William Tecumseh Sherman's Union troops burned every home on the river during their march north from Georgia. The story maintains that Drayton was saved because its occupant, a doctor, posted yellow flags around the property signaling its use as a smallpox hospital. Another tradition suggests that a Northern cousin in the Union navy blockade nearby used his influence to save his relative's property. According to my tour guide, relatively little is known about the

Drayton family's life at the house. No inventories exist. Many of the family's papers were lost during the Civil War and few pieces of original furniture remain. Yet, little by little, the secrets of the past are uncovered as the staff continue to do their research.

President Madison's Home Reborn

Drayton is perhaps a rare example of a historic house with little change over time. Most houses change constantly with a stream of occupants who update them to keep current with styles and modern technology. President James Madison's home Montpelier, another National Trust property, sits in the rolling countryside of Piedmont Virginia. It opened to the public in the mid-1980s when its last owner donated it to the trust. Montpelier offers an interesting example of the challenge of interpretation. Throughout the decades its owners had altered its appearance and it looked nothing like it did when James and Dolley built it. The last owners, the duPonts, doubled the size, the additions completely altering the Madison core. The majority of visitors come to visit the house because of its Madison association, but the duPont floorplan had made interpretation problematic since so little was left of the original design. The Madison story was lost within a house that illustrated a different story. For years there was a debate about whether or not to restore the house to its original appearance. This would require extensive research, funds, and demolition. After research determined that enough physical evidence existed to accurately portray the Madison story, the board decided to carefully bring back the Madison house and allow visitors to watch the transformation. A five-year $25 million building effort restored the house to its 1820 appearance. Because the property's furniture collection reflects the later owners, the curators began a worldwide search to locate and purchase original furniture from the Madison period. Today a visitor to the property learns not only about the Madisons but also about the fascinating process of restoring the property.

Five Families, One House

The Ipswich house at the American History Museum is a good example of change. As the museum's staff researched the house's history, they discovered that at least eighty-six people had lived there. Who were they? How did they change the house over time? None of them are familiar to Americans today. Yet in many ways their stories mirror the history of America. The new exhibition would tell those stories and encourage visitors to think about their own homes as historical sources. And by exploring various source materials that revealed clues about the Ipswich house, visitors could learn how to research their own homes.

From the start there were huge challenges. First, the artifact's fragile condition did not allow millions of visitors per year to enter the house; second, the limited space available for the exhibition did not allow for a ramp or access to view the building's second floor. So the developers needed to figure out how to draw visitors into the story while they walked around the outside of the first level. Finally, while most of the house had been transported from Massachusetts, a third of it had not. The plan was to create the illusion of the entire house by hinting at the end section that wasn't there using an obvious framework.

The curators who did the research and wrote the main exhibition text chose to focus on five families who lived in the house and to create vignettes, with minimal furniture, to help visitors imagine the house as it changed over time. With the house as the primary focal point, the family stories were interwoven throughout, showing how their circumstances transformed the house and how the context of the neighborhood changed. Since the house could not talk, the stories would be told through historical evidence.

Abraham Choate, a miller and maritime merchant, built the house in the 1760s to reflect his growing wealth. While better off than most of their neighbors, Abraham and his wife, Sarah, were not among the colony's elite. The house's appearance announced that the Choates were on their way up the prosperity ladder. The parlor tells their story. This public room where the Choates entertained guests had wallpapered walls with paneling and ornate plaster work. Neighbors visiting for tea might sit on an elegant hand-carved side chair. The master of the house wore silver buckles on his shoes and his daughters played with fashionable dolls. By 1772, when he sold the house, Choate identified himself in the deed as a "gentleman."

In 1777, during the American Revolution, another Abraham, Abraham Dodge, bought the house. He and his second wife, Bethiah, lived in the house through the 1780s. The hallway represented their wealth with its expensive green paint and elaborate stair rail. The curators referred to the hallway as a sorting chamber—only visitors of a certain status came through the front door and were received by the family. Some ended up in the parlor, while those closest to the family might go upstairs for tea in the bedchambers. Servants and workmen would call at the rear of the house. During the Revolutionary War, Dodge enlisted as a captain in the Massachusetts militia and his company fought at the Battle of Bunker Hill. While not much is known about the Dodges' life in the house, the researchers uncovered evidence that an African American man named Chance lived with the family. The door to the attic in a nearby exhibit case reflects his position as a servant in the family—he most likely slept in the unheated attic. Dodge's 1786 will indicates that he bequeathed to his wife the services of his "Negro man Chance." Slavery had ended in Massachusetts by then, but Chance remained caught in the transition to freedom.

Josiah and Lucy Caldwell bought the house in 1822. A family of reformers, they were leaders in the antislavery movement of the time. Josiah, a singing teacher, owned an ornate square piano that he used for antislavery sing-alongs in a second parlor, which tells their story. When they purchased the house it was more than fifty years old, so they remodeled its facade into the popular Greek Revival style and modernized the interior, covering the paneling with wallpaper and plaster and adding new technology—stoves in the fireplaces. Newspaper ads show that Lucy hosted meetings of the Ipswich Female Anti Slavery Society in her parlor, while Josiah led the Ipswich Anti Slavery Society. While it can't be documented, perhaps several famous abolitionists passed through the house.

By the 1870s, the neighborhood had transformed into an industrial mill district and was no longer fashionable. The area was home to many new immigrants and the house was converted into two apartments. An Irish immigrant named Catherine Lynch and her daughter Mary rented one side of the house. Mary worked at the local mills making cotton stockings while Catherine, a middle-aged widow, did laundry to earn a living and pay her part of the $50 annual rent. One of the parlors became a kitchen and residents of both apartments shared an outhouse in the backyard. Catherine's kitchen and yard were her workplace. The house was over one hundred years old and its modest rooms reflected the working class status of its residents.

The exhibition team wanted to tell the Lynches' story but did not have a room to feature. Thus we decided to use the yard to portray her work as a laundress. In an attempt to convey the difficult backbreaking work, we came up with a unique concept that allowed visitors to try their hand at doing the laundry—we called it the "wring-o-meter." A visitor grasped two handles and turned a piece of laundry to simulate the wringing process. An arrow moving on a scale of wet to dry indicated the strength of the movement, allowing the visitor to compare his success against Mrs. Lynch's. A clothesline of laundry contained text outlining the laundering process. Nearby stood a bucket weighing twenty-one pounds, equivalent to two gallons of water. By lifting the bucket a few times, a visitor could quickly understand the strength required to lift twenty-five buckets to complete just one load of laundry.

Walking clockwise around the house, visitors to the exhibition finally came to a kitchen. The curators decided to use the kitchen to tell the story of the Scotts, a family who lived in the house during World War II. The house was still divided into two apartments, but by this time one was upstairs and one downstairs. In many ways the kitchen was the center of family life. It was heated by a coal and wood cooking range. Roy Scott installed the house's first indoor toilet in the mid-1940s. Mary Scott was the family's matriarch and her two sons Roy and Arthur served in the military. Mary moved into the house with her daughter Annie, son-in-law Richard, and a young grandson, Dicky. Annie made proximity fuses for antiaircraft projectiles in the nearby Sylvania factory where the old Ipswich mills had stood. Mary spent much time in the kitchen canning vegetables from the family's victory garden and supporting the war effort. The room's thick blackout shades reflected the dangerous times.

The final section of the exhibition showed some of the ways that historians researched the Ipswich house. From documents like census records, insurance maps, and city directories, to paint samples, floor joists, and panel sections, there are many clues that tell the house's stories. Another source was the people who lived in the house. Richard S. Lynch, Mary Scott's grandson, provided much information about growing up in the Ipswich house. He was amazed that his family's home is in the Smithsonian. In a poignant visit, he brought his own grandson to the exhibition's opening and showed him where he had grown up. He is probably the only person who can say that his childhood house is in the Smithsonian.

Not surprisingly, exhibition developers and fabricators take great pride in their work. By the time the Ipswich house exhibition officially opened as "Within These Walls . . ." in the spring of 2001, more than fifty people had been involved in the project. An exhibition that size takes years to research, develop, and build. While this exhibition included a credit panel, the staff also found an innovative way to leave their mark. The fabrication crew had recreated a portion of the backyard, which included an outhouse. The door to the outhouse was open a few inches. Before the door was nailed into place, exhibition team members signed their names on the inside. Though there was no fanfare, it was a thrilling moment accompanied by the sense of achievement that comes with the completion of a challenging task.

It's one outhouse I'm glad to have my name in.

10
WATER
BATTLE ON
THE MISSOURI

The charge of the expedition is honorable
to myself as it is important to my country.

—*Meriwether Lewis*

Years ago a man was deciding whether or not to leave his government job in Washington DC to travel to the Western Country . . . to
unknown lands. It would be a journey through Native tribes that he
assured his mother would be perfectly friendly. As he told her: "The
charge of the expedition is honorable to myself, as it is important to
my country. For its fatigues I feel myself perfectly prepared nor do
I doubt my health and strength of constitution to bear me through
it." He decided to go, with "the most perfect preconviction in my
own mind of returning safe." Those are the words of Meriwether
Lewis to his mother in a letter dated July 2, 1803. In a small way
they reflect my story.

One day in September 2001 I woke up in St. Louis, eight hundred
miles west of Washington and in some ways thousands of miles

from all I held dear. I wasn't in Smithsonianland anymore. What had caused me to pick up and leave a secure federal position at the pinnacle of the museum world and move to a place that barely registers in the thoughts of an Easterner? It was Lewis and Clark fever, a dangerous history bug. I had accepted a position at the Missouri Historical Society as project educator on a team charged with developing a traveling exhibition about the Lewis and Clark expedition in commemoration of its bicentennial (2004–2006). In short, the opportunity to work on a high-profile national traveling exhibition was too good to pass up.

My decision took me on a fascinating journey into a Western world brimming with present-day tension, one inhabited by both Lewis and Clark fanatics, passionate about the expedition and its place in America's history, and a variety of tribal groups determined to speak truth about the expedition's legacy. I stepped into this world after an innocent but transformational encounter with the explorers on their trail in Montana.

During my entire school career in Pennsylvania I read only a few paragraphs about Meriwether Lewis and William Clark in history classes. I knew who they were, of course, but their story had not captured my imagination, perhaps because I had never traveled west. I was not even aware that Meriwether Lewis had stopped in my hometown, Lancaster, to meet with astronomer Andrew Ellicott on his way to Philadelphia while planning the expedition in 1803. One day, while working at the American History Museum, I caught the Lewis and Clark bug. A book group I belonged to had read Stephen Ambrose's *Undaunted Courage* and invited a Smithsonian scholar and his Mandan (North Dakota Native) friend to join our discussion of the book. Their tales of adventures along the Lewis and Clark trail piqued my curiosity.

The Trail West

Shortly after that, I happily seized an opportunity to accompany a Smithsonian study tour along the expedition's route in western

Montana and Idaho. The eighteen-member group from across the nation gathered at Great Falls, Montana, on a hot day in August. My job as the Smithsonian representative and host of the group was to ensure that everyone had a good time and that the trip went smoothly. This was my first time in Montana and my immediate concern was fire: it was fire season and wild fires raged in parts of the state. I feared that road closures due to fires would affect our itinerary, and I did not want anything to spoil this trip.

Ranging in age from eighteen to mid-seventies, our group members came from every region of the country, but our common fascination with the Lewis and Clark expedition led to a powerful bonding experience. Since we were bravely following in Lewis and Clark's footsteps, what better way to begin the trip than with a hot (in the hundreds) afternoon float trip down the Missouri River? We put in east of the series of dams and power plants that have totally altered the spectacle that Lewis saw. In Great Falls today, it takes a powerful imagination to envision the river as it appeared two hundred years ago.

In this ten-mile stretch of river, Lewis and the expedition encountered five waterfalls, the tallest he estimated to be eighty feet high. Lewis described it as "the grandest sight I ever beheld." He rhapsodized about "the perfect white foam which assumes a thousand forms in a moment sometimes flying up in jets of sparkling foam to the height of fifteen or twenty feet." What was beautiful to behold quickly became a nightmare to portage around. The expedition members carried and pushed and dragged the dugouts along an eighteen-mile path around the falls.

Our three rafts drifted with the current through the desolate countryside east of the city of Great Falls, the scenery virtually unchanged over two hundred years. The land appears barren and rocky, yet long grasses cover its rolling hills. We tried to imagine what Lewis or Clark might have thought of this alien landscape. In the expedition journals Lewis described the "beauty of this majestically grand scenery." He also noted huge herds of elk and antelope and especially buffalo. Clark estimated one herd of buffalo numbered near ten thousand. On June 13, 1805, Lewis wrote, "From the extremity of this rolling country, I overlooked a most beautiful and level plain of great extent or at least 50 or 60 miles; in this there were infinitely more buffalo than I had ever before witnessed at a view." This abundance of animals meant the expedition members were eating well. Lewis called his meal that night sumptuous—it included buffalo hump, tongue, and marrowbone and fine trout. Sadly, today the barren beauty of the landscape testifies to the tragic disappearance of the great animal herds. We could only see part of the awesome scene that spread before the expedition members' eyes.

Yet all was not beauty and sweetness on this part of the river, and numerous challenges assaulted the men. One was animals. Grizzlies were such a problem that the captains would not send a man out on an errand alone. On July 14, 1804, Lewis himself confronted one of the bears. He was alone and had just encountered a herd of a thousand buffalo. After he shot one he realized that a bear had crept up to within twenty steps of him. As he drew his gun to defend himself, he remembered that he had forgotten to reload. When the bear charged him, Lewis quickly assessed his surroundings—not a tree in sight. Running into the river up to his waist, he faced the bear head on, an espontoon (a long wooden pole with a metal spearlike tip) his only weapon. He later recorded that the bear stopped twenty feet from him at the edge of the water. "The moment I put myself in this attitude of defense he suddenly wheeled about as if frightened, declined to combat on such unequal grounds, and retreated with quite as great precipitation as he had just before pursued me."

But Lewis's encounters with animals that day were not over. He next saw what he first thought was a wolf, but quickly decided it was a cat "of the tiger kind." Historian Stephen Ambrose writes that it was probably a wolverine. The animal crouched, ready to pounce. Lewis took aim and fired, but it disappeared into its burrow. "It now seemed to me that all the beasts of the neighborhood had made a league to destroy me, or that some fortune was disposed to amuse herself at my expense." He had not proceeded three hundred yards when three buffalo bulls separated from a nearby herd and charged him at full speed. They halted at a hundred yards. He had planned to spend the night separated from the rest of the expedition, but "did not think it prudent to remain all night at this place which really from the succession of curious adventures wore the impression on my mind of enchantment; at sometimes for a moment I thought it might be a dream."

Besides animals, other challenges included prickly pear cactus with sharp spikes that jabbed through the moccasins and caused much damage to the men's feet, and rattlesnakes, which Clark described as innumerable, "requir[ing] great caution to prevent being bitten." And one phrase appears over and over in the journals at this point in the expedition: the "mosquitoes are extremely troublesome to us."

To add to the misery, members of the party were having health problems. Two men complained of a toothache, three men had "tumors," and one a slight fever; and Sacagawea, the Indian woman who accompanied the expedition with her baby, was extremely ill. As doctor of the group, Lewis kept busy providing various remedies. He was most worried about Sacagawea—the party desperately needed her to negotiate with the Shoshone Indians for horses later on in the expedition. But despite doses of bark and opium, she continued to experience pain in the lower abdomen. The men found a sulfur spring and Lewis resolved to test its healing qualities on Sacagawea.

Our party decided to stop at the spring. We paddled the rafts over to the riverbank and traipsed through the dried grass to the spring. The water still smells slightly of rotten eggs and remains surprisingly untouched by humanity, probably because it sits surrounded by a rattlesnake habitat. I could easily picture one of the expedition members filling a canteen with the mineral water and taking it to Lewis, who poured it down Sacagawea's throat. The sulfur water was apparently a miracle cure because the following day she was much better, free of pain and fever, her pulse regular, and her appetite returned. The stinky sulfur spring we were staring at had saved Sacagawea's life.

We continued down the river. As I gazed at the stretch ahead, my reverie was interrupted by a blast of water hitting my leg. Suddenly a torrent of water sprayed the boat, followed by howling laughter. Our raft was under attack! At the instigation of their guide, several people in one of the other rafts had gleefully picked up the huge water guns stored for use on hot days. I unexpectedly found myself in the middle of a water battle. The attackers had an average age of about sixty-five, were financially well off, educated, and well read—not the type of foes that one expects to face in battle. The heat had apparently pushed them over the edge. I was quickly soaked, and my first instinct was to jump in and defend myself, but I reconsidered my involvement. I concluded that as a representative of the Smithsonian, I should watch my moves. I looked over at our study leader, who was sitting nearby and getting hit in the face. He grinned and shrugged and we both decided to enjoy the coolness of the water. I quickly identified the ringleader—one middle-aged lady, a gleam in her eye and a large water machine gun in her hand.

During that week the group experienced other adventures: swimming in Lolo hot springs; camping in tents high in the Bitterroot Mountains in Idaho; hiking on the Lolo trail on steep pine hillsides; canoeing down the Clearwater River through smoke-filled ridges; and staying overnight in Salmon, Idaho, where the ashes from a nearby wild fire fell around us. A horseback ride to the Smoking Place proved a truly spiritual experience for me. This stunning vista in the Bitterroots is where the expedition stopped on June 27, 1806, on their return journey. Clark wrote, "[W]e halted by the request of the Guides a few minutes on an elevated point and smoked a pipe. From this place we had an extensive view of these stupendous mountains principally covered with snow like that on which we stood. We were entirely surrounded by those mountains from which, to one unacquainted with them, it would have seemed impossible ever to have escaped in short without the assistance of our guides, I doubt much whether we who had once passed them could find our way to Travelers Rest. . . . After having smoked the pipe and contemplating this scene sufficient to have dampened the spirits of any except such hardy travelers as we have become, we continued our march."

Our own descent from that place became an exercise in faith for me. The horses' hooves stirred up clouds of dust that made it impossible to see the next step of the steep, rocky trail. I had no choice but to trust my horse. With a bandana around my face to catch the dust, I felt like a true Westerner.

The Power of the Landscape

At camp that evening, after I washed up in the freezing water hole and beat one of our van drivers in a game of horseshoes, I stared up into the vastness of the star-strewn Idaho sky. Little did I know then that I was being drawn into a drama that captivates thousands who travel the Lewis and Clark trail every year. Despite the heat and mosquitoes and smoke, the power of this landscape had reignited my fascination for history in a new way. This wasn't Williamsburg, a carefully crafted civilized immersion in place and time. This was an immersion of timelessness, of raw land. Like my fellow travelers on that trip and future trips, my appreciation for what Lewis and Clark's expedition accomplished was greater because, in a minute but tangible way, I'd experienced their struggles and their awe in traversing this landscape.

There is a power in history that is palpable. If cultivated, it can affect even the person who claims no interest in history. Every day I witness the intrinsic power of the real stuff—objects, documents, photographs, and maps—as visitors gaze with awe at America's treasures. But place holds its own kind of power. Many people are overcome with emotion at Pearl Harbor or on the beaches of Normandy. For me, there are many places that evoke the voices from the past. Antietam battlefield, for example, or Thomas Jefferson's home Monticello. The view from the garden pavilion at Monticello over the south orchard to the mountains beyond is sublime. Harpers Ferry, West Virginia, continues to draw me back time and time again, and I can almost hear the shouts and shots as I picture John Brown's raid on the arsenal there. Or Charleston, South Carolina, one of my favorite American cities. The sense of history permeates the heavy Southern air.

But of all the historical places I have visited, one stands above the rest: Lemhi Pass, the mountain pass over the continental divide at the Montana/Idaho state line high in the Bitterroot Mountains. Here Lewis stood in awe of the never-ending mountain ridges rising before him and realized the huge challenge ahead. Today, the spot remains in a pristine state of wildness. I've been there three times, and every time its desolation and sweeping vistas transport my mind back to August 1805 when Lewis wrote, "[W]e proceeded on to the top of the dividing ridge from which I discovered immense ranges of high mountains still to the West of us with their tops partially covered with snow."

Nearby is the source of the Missouri River—where a small gurgle of water gushes from the ground. On one trip to this spot my traveling companions were a mixed group of whites and American Indians, all teachers from reservation schools. Near the area where Lewis and a few of his party went on ahead to find the Shoshone Indians, I found myself with two new friends of Shoshone-Bannock heritage. Straddling the narrow stream where the water pours from the ground and meanders down a hill to eventually become the Missouri River, we tasted the water and wondered at the journey it would take. Lewis called it "the most distant fountain of the waters of the mighty Missouri, in search of which we have spent so many toilsome days and restless nights." He wrote that expedition member McNeal had "exultingly stood with a foot on each side of this little rivulet and thanked his god that he had lived to bestride the mighty and heretofore deemed endless Missouri." As I do at times, I decided to find a small stone to take with me, a symbol to remember the moment. However, I tend not to label the rocks from my travels and now find myself with a pile of them, each filled with a meaning lost to a foggy memory. (My friends think I'm crazy, especially those who have helped me move.)

My companions that day saw me take a pebble and thought it a good idea. They, too, each picked up a small pebble. We were on our way to join up with the rest of our group when one of the teachers stopped. She felt in her pockets, dug something out, and turned back. Curious, I watched as she unwrapped a piece of hard candy and placed it at the spot where she had picked up her pebble. She explained to me later that her people believe that when you take something, you need to put something else in its place. I pondered this for a bit—in theory I liked the practice, and hard candy for a pebble seemed a perfect exchange. The candy would quickly melt and leave the spot as natural as before. As I delved deeper into the various cultural traditions of different Western Indian tribes, I gained an appreciation for these rich and complex cultures. The Lewis and Clark story, as I soon learned, is not only about their encounters with the natural landscape, but with the cultural landscape as well.

The Path of an Exhibition

The National Lewis and Clark Bicentennial Exhibition could have gone in any number of directions. In the past, most interpretations of the story concentrated on the expedition's journey through the natural landscape—of conquering rapids, bad weather, heat, dust, hail, grizzlies, mosquitoes, and storms—and hailed the expedition's discoveries of new plants and animals. When I first met Carolyn Gilman, curator of the exhibition, I quickly learned that this exhibition would not take a traditional path. Two hundred years after the the original voyage, the time was right for a different look at the story. This time, Carolyn was determined to focus on the cultural landscape. Doubtless this approach would not have worked even one hundred years before. In 1904 America's battles with the Native nations were fresh in everyone's memory. The early twentieth century was the low point of Indian existence in the United States. They were forced to live on reservations and send their children to boarding schools, and were forbidden to practice their religions and speak their languages. Most Americans thought the Native people were doomed to extinction. But in 2004, with recent scholarly emphasis on social and minority history, an exhibition that looked at several perspectives, including a women's perspective and Native perspectives, could serve to provoke thought and maybe even help to correct surprising public misconceptions—like the fact that not all American Indians had been killed off.

When Carolyn described the exhibition, she liked to say it was not only about the view from the river but also the view from the riverbank. Of course, there wasn't just one view from the riverbank as there wasn't just one river. On the journey to the Pacific Ocean and back, the expedition made contact with at least fifty-five tribes and most likely passed through the tribal lands of even more. How would we tell the stories of the many Native tribes that encountered Lewis and Clark? Carolyn decided to concentrate on six tribes. She also made a decision early on to present these stories within a thematic context based on the expedition's encounters. Therefore, the diplomacy theme focused on the early encounters with the Teton Sioux, a meeting that resulted in a tense standoff that almost ended the expedition. The mapping and women themes focused on the Mandan Indians. The warrior and language themes focused on the Shoshone. The healing and plant section focused on the Nez Perce, and the trade and property theme focused on the Chinook.

In the three years that I spent working on the Lewis and Clark exhibition I had numerous opportunities to gain a deeper understanding of Native cultures and as a result, the expedition's story became much more vivid to me. My travels on the Lewis and Clark trail and my cross-cultural exchanges were not that different from my earlier experiences in Williamsburg as a child. My passion had once again dramatically increased about a historical topic because my senses had been engaged and my mind could imagine a different time and place. The experience, though, was profoundly different because Native cultures are alive and well. I would soon learn that their past connects in deep and profound ways to their future.

11
YOU CAN'T WRITE MY HISTORY

History is written by the winners, they say. But
it is often the losers who care more about it.

—*Carolyn Gilman*

"You cannot write our story. You have no right." An irate Indian
woman had backed me into a corner. She was not yelling, but she
was passionate. We were standing in a classroom on the University
of Montana campus in Missoula. Our group consisted of teachers,
Indian and non-Indian, from reservation schools in seven Western
and Midwestern states, plus those of us who had planned the trip.
The Center for Educational Technology in Indian America, an arm
of the Bureau of Indian Affairs, had organized the seminar to kick
off a project to encourage Indian students to research their tribe's
and community's perspective on the Lewis and Clark expedition
and to make the results available to the public. We were following a section of the Lewis and Clark trail in western Montana. We

planners recognized that not every participant would have a positive impression of Lewis and Clark. How would they react? Would there be uncomfortable moments? There was a slight amount of trepidation that the workshop would fail.

An Introduction to Native Cultures

I came to the Lewis and Clark project with limited experience working with American Indians. While at the American History Museum I had worked on an online project about buffalo hide paintings, but I had not had significant contact with Native communities. When I joined the Lewis and Clark project I was quickly thrown into Native culture. I subscribed to the *Indian Country Today* weekly newspaper and soon began to interact with Native Americans or Indians or . . . Actually, the first big question many non-Indians ask is about proper terminology. On the politically correct East Coast, the term one most often hears is "Native American." However, I soon learned that in the West the preferred term is "American Indian." Ultimately, I came to understand that one should use a specific tribal name when known. On occasion I will have non-Indian people try to correct me or even ask me what term they should use . . . they think "Indian" is not a sensitive word. I usually point out that the Smithsonian museum devoted to Native cultures is called the National Museum of the American Indian, a name given it by the Native peoples themselves.

Including the Native perspective in the exhibition proved a challenge in part because of the unbalanced historical record. Today we know so much about the expedition because President Jefferson instructed Lewis and Clark to keep journals, and fortunately these journals have survived. The explorers documented their activities and observations on the expedition with attention to detail and have been called the "writingest explorers of their time." Yet it is also important to remember that the men of the Corps of Discovery made observations through a very specific lens, a lens based on their experience as white men. Lewis and Clark looked through the eyes of men who had grown up in privileged families. The others on the expedition, including Clark's slave, York, no doubt had very different observations.

The Indian cultures that Lewis and Clark encountered did not record history through written documentation but through three main media: pictographs, artwork on objects such as buffalo hides, and oral tradition. Very little evidence of Lewis and Clark is available from the first two sources. However, fascinating stories about the expedition have been passed down through oral tradition in certain tribes. A Salish woman named Sophie Moiesse told a story that was recorded in the early 1900s. "When the dried meat was brought to the men [the Corps of Discovery] they just looked at it and put it back. It was really good to eat, but they seemed to think it was bark or wood. Also, they didn't know that camas roots are good to eat." Allen Pinkham, Nez Perce, tells about the councils held to discuss the expedition. "Well if they bring too many bad things, maybe we should kill them. Well, let's treat these people good once. Maybe they're mixed with some other creature that's why they look the way they do. They've got eyes like fish; some of them have their faces upside down, and they smell." Eyes like fish referred to their round shape. Face upside down referred to mustaches and beards and limited hair on top. Pinkham continues that "we couldn't understand why they called themselves white when they're really not white. They're pale, that's the way we described them."

Bring In the Advisers

To accurately include the Native perspective, the exhibition developers understood that we needed tribal advisers to provide counsel during the research and planning phases. My responsibilities included organizing a meeting of tribal advisers. The goal was to find representatives from the main tribes featured in the exhibition and to bring them together from around the country for a weekend meeting. Some of these advisers were already involved in the project. For those tribes with which we had not already established a relationship, the task proved somewhat of a challenge. I quickly learned that it can be difficult to find an Indian who is willing to speak for his or her tribe. Few people in Indian communities have that authority. Combine that fact with the distasteful nature of what we were trying to do (commemorate Lewis and Clark), and it's easy to see why certain Indians did not want to be involved.

The hardest person to find, ironically, was a Shoshone representative. The tribe today is divided into three groups, two in Idaho and one in Wyoming. We ended up with a very nice person from the wrong group. Most scholars would agree that the Shoshones on the Wind River Reservation in Wyoming probably have the weakest connection to Lewis and Clark. However, just as Lewis and Clark desperately needed to find the Shoshone in order to obtain horses to cross the Bitterroot Mountains before winter set in, we desperately needed a Shoshone to advise us on several major sections of the exhibition and our time was running out. While we did include a Shoshone representative at the meeting, our adviser from Wind River proved eager but not familiar with the oral tradition related to Lewis and Clark. Eight months later, as we prepared to film a movie for the exhibition, we made an excellent connection to several women from the Lemhi Shoshone who claim direct descendancy from the family of Sacagawea, the Indian woman who traveled with the expedition. These advisers were more than willing to work with our film crew to ensure accuracy. The film highlighted the narrative of the expedition's necessity of finding the Shoshone and the challenges associated with communication once they found them. In the end many Indians of Shoshone ancestry proved to be very helpful in our efforts.

The ten tribal advisers traveled to St. Louis from Alaska, Washington DC, and many places in between. They were willing to work with us so that the truth would be told and their tribe's perspective of the story would be represented. The exhibition team spent a long day going through the concept plan for the exhibition and looking at images of specific Indian artifacts we planned to include. For the most part the advisers were eager to talk about the artifacts and approved our planned interpretations.

The Realm of the Pipe

One of the most interesting discussions centered around the concept of the "peace pipe." Historian James Ronda calls Indian country "the realm of the pipe" and says that Lewis and Clark encountered the pipe in its many forms and faces. There is a common perception in American culture, fostered in many a Hollywood Western, that Indians smoked the pipe with others to diplomatically promote peaceful relations, as an act of friendship. Very quickly in our discussion various advisers spoke out. One said that her tribe does not have a "peace" pipe—she described the pipe ceremony as a very sacred ceremony to promote truth among the witnessing spirits . . . a sort of "truth pipe" to encourage everyone present to speak truthfully.

We hoped to feature a very exquisite calumet pipe from the late 1700s or early 1800s from the collection of the Peabody Museum of Archeology and Ethnography at Harvard University. Research revealed there was a high probability it was one of several given to Lewis during the expedition as a gift. Ronda wrote that "the pipe ritual aimed at clearing the air, quieting the mind, and making space for peace. Smoking sacred pipes united the social and the diplomatic, the personal and the official." Lewis and Clark experienced pipes as social and diplomatic objects, and as gifts. William Clark wrote his observations: "The pipe is the emblem of peace with all, the different nations have their different fashions of delivering and receiving of it—the party delivering generally confess their errors and request a peace, the party receiving exult in their successes and receive the sacred stem."

We also planned to include Lewis's personal pipe tomahawk, with a pipe at one end and a tomahawk at the other. The pipe tomahawk was unique to the American frontier and originated around 1700. It combined the Indian pipe of peace and the European ax of war, and was symbolic of encounters in the West. Every encounter required both parties to quickly decide whether the other was friend of foe. To one of our advisers, the very act of putting a pipe and tomahawk into one tool was troubling. To her, a pipe is sacred and has nothing to do with war.

With the advisers' blessing, the exhibition featured the calumet pipe and the Lewis pipe tomahawk. A majority of the advisers had given a nod to the pipe tomahawk, and the developers incorporated the different perspectives into the Web site and student curriculum.

Speaking from the Heart

Another item on the agenda that day was filming interviews with the advisers. We had given them questions ahead of time and mostly wanted them to speak about their tribe's oral traditions related to Lewis and Clark and how they personally felt about the expedition and the bicentennial. We also attempted to ask them about topics of interest related to what they had said earlier in the day. My experience interviewing them that day was one of the highlights of my time working on the project. The advisers spoke with passion, their words personal, profound, and deeply moving. They talked about the loss of Native languages, the misperceptions people have about Native cultures, the unfairness of federal tribal recognition, and of survival amid much adversity. As I reviewed the footage later, I was struck by the depth of what they had shared with us. I determined to find a way to use this footage in the exhibition.

Early on in discussions about the exhibition's final section, the team had considered using a montage of Indian voices talking about the expedition's impact on Native culture then and now. I had envisioned something like what has been done at the U.S. Holocaust Memorial Museum in Washington, where the visitor experience ends with a room filled with monitors playing video of survivors sharing their heartbreaking yet inspiring stories. Sadly, in the end we cut the montage idea, mainly because of space limitations. It was a loss born of compromise, the nature of exhibitions. Fortunately, we were able to make use of the video segments in the online exhibition and in the curriculum, but we could not include some of the most profound parts.

From my interactions with the advisers I learned much about who has the right to tell history. There is clearly no one Indian history any more than there is one American Indian. While movies and advertisements and pop culture have attempted to generalize about Native Americans over the years, there are 561 federally recognized tribes in the United States, and even more than that number are not officially recognized. The perpetual and pervasive image of the Plains Indian in feathered headdress on horseback has made hundreds of thousands of Indians cringe over the years because it has nothing to do with their cultures.

Developing the extensive grades 4–12 curriculum materials that went along with the exhibition was my responsibility. My plan was to work with Carolyn and closely follow the exhibition narrative, using the objects and oral histories from the exhibit. My past experience had shown me that it is easiest for someone who knows the exhibition well to write the curriculum. Thus, during my trip to Montana, I ended up with the irate Indian woman in my face. She told me in no uncertain terms that I couldn't write the curriculum about the Indian experience because I am not Indian. I tried to explain that a curriculum based on an exhibition usually highlights the interpretation in the exhibition and should allow the students to work directly with the primary source material. The objects speak for themselves. Plus, the exhibition team intended to use Native reviewers and advisers along the way. I could not change her mind.

But she raised some thoughtful questions. Who owns history? Can we own our culture's story? Can we own our personal story? Who has the right to tell what story? Can an African American tell the story of a white plantation owner in the antebellum South? Can a Sioux researcher tell the story of Booker T. Washington? Must our skin color dictate the history we tell? For most of my museum career I've navigated a very political world where whites must tread carefully through the stories of the past. Emotions can run high. And maybe that's the key to the answer—historians can analyze the evidence and draw conclusions, but they can't ultimately say how a person truly felt during the event or as a result. The most powerful storyteller is usually the person who has experienced the story firsthand. We all have a story and we are the person that can tell it best. Historian Eric Foner once wrote, "Who owns history? Everyone and no one—which is why the study of the past is a constantly evolving, never-ending journey of discovery."

Who Was Sacagawea?

After Lewis and Clark, the person most often associated with the expedition is Sacagawea, the Indian woman who joined the party in the spring of 1805 when the captains hired her husband as a translator. She wasn't a paid member of the expedition party. She had given birth to a baby boy, Jean Baptiste, in February and brought the baby along when the Corps of Discovery left the Mandan village in May. Her role on the expedition is often misunderstood; while her "story" has been told in countless books, the truth rests on scarce historical evidence. The exhibition team members were well aware of this challenge but realized that visitors would expect to see her story in the exhibition. When we were developing the exhibition, she was the only expedition member whose likeness had appeared on U.S. currency—the dollar coin (though no historical evidence offers great detail about her appearance). She remains a mystery in history—an almost unknown yet legendary figure. Little physical evidence remains to tell us much about her and today, a swirl of Indian oral tradition cannot even agree on her tribal heritage. Some Hidatsa Indians claim she was Hidatsa, captured by the Shoshone. Most Shoshone say it is clear she was Shoshone and that the Lewis and Clark journals support this. Unfortunately she did not leave even one piece of written evidence about her life. She cannot tell her story.

A Tribal Elder Talks

During the development of the exhibition I took a research trip to central North Dakota to visit the Knife River Indian Villages National Historic Site. Located not far from the Missouri River, the site was the location of the summer villages of the Mandan and Hidatsa peoples, farming tribes who lived in round earth lodges. I went specifically to see the Northern Plains Indian Cultural Fest, an annual event that includes atlatl throwing, beadworking, porcupine quill work, brain tanning, hide painting, flute music, flint knapping, basketry, rock art, and talks by various tribal elders and guest speakers.

At 11:00 a.m. I joined a small crowd seated on folding chairs under a white tent. At the front of the tent sat an eighty-eight-year-old Arikara elder in full regalia—feathered headdress covering his dark hair. August Little Soldier, one of the oldest living of the Three Affiliated Tribes (Mandan, Hidatsa, and Arikara), began a rambling talk about his life and his observations of the world. His family heritage connected him to the Battle of Little Bighorn; his grandfather had died with Custer and as a scout had warned Custer not to attack. Little Soldier traveled down a winding path of topics—the origins of the Hidatsa (from the east in Minnesota) and the Arikara (branch of the Pawnee from Oklahoma), a World War I navy ship named the *Arikara*, an observation that Christianity is going "downhill" and that Christians cannot find a way to unite. He talked about his marriage of sixty-four years to a German woman and the fact that he is full blooded and went to boarding school. At the end of his talk he offered to answer questions from the audience. I inquired about Arikara oral tradition related to Lewis and Clark. To my great surprise he responded matter-of-factly that Clark fell in love with Sacagawea and took her to Washington DC after the expedition, where he wanted to introduce her to high society. She apparently did not want that life and returned to the West. I hadn't heard this story before and was suspicious. I looked around the audience to see if others showed surprise. Was he pulling my leg, this white person showing an interest in Lewis and Clark, or did he really believe this version of Sacagawea's story? I questioned my hosts at a picnic that night. They laughed but didn't give me a clear answer.

The Evidence for Sacagawea

The Lewis and Clark journals mention Sacagawea seventy-three times. The explorers first met Sacagawea, Sacajawea, or Sakakawea (the pronunciation varies according to tribal affiliation) in the fall of 1804. A pregnant teenager, she was a wife of Toussaint Charbonneau, an interpreter offering his skills to the captains. Lewis and Clark wrote that she was a Shoshone girl who had been captured by the Hidatsa in a war raid and taken to the Knife River villages. It is curious to consider why Lewis and Clark would bother to take a new mother and child along on the expedition. They recognized her language skills and knew they would need to find and communicate with the Shoshones in order to obtain horses to cross the mountains. She was no doubt more important to them in this regard than her husband.

Contrary to popular legend, Sacagawea was not the expedition's guide, though the journals reveal her various contributions to the group. She helped them identify edible plants like wild artichokes along the way and gathered root foods, which provided a balanced diet. When the corps finally reached her tribe's homeland, she recognized various landmarks, such as a rock formation shaped like a beaver's head, that could confirm their location. Once, during a boating accident, she saved provisions and some of the journals that had fallen from the boat. In addition, her presence communicated to Indian scouts that the expedition was not a war party, since a war party would not include a woman and child. Popular images picture her alongside the captains, hand outstretched pointing the way as if she were giving them directions to a restaurant. In reality, since they spoke different languages, Sacagawea and members of the expedition could not communicate directly. Most likely they gradually learned words from each other's language, but the majority of time her messages were translated through a series of interpreters—until it reached the English speakers.

The journals reveal little about Sacagawea's personality, though Lewis and Clark both grew to respect her greatly, praising her "fortitude and resolution" and her patience. In what must have been one of the emotional highlights of the expedition, Sacagawea participated in a council with the Shoshone chief, Cameahwait, preparing to serve as translator. When she recognized him as her brother, according to Clark, she "instantly jumped up, and ran and embraced him, throwing over him her blanket and weeping profusely." During the party's stay on the Pacific coast a whale washed up on shore and Sacagawea insisted on going to see it. Lewis wrote that "the Indian woman was very importunate to be permitted to go, and was therefore indulged."

Clark clearly thought highly of Sacagawea and her son, Baptiste, who he named Pomp. He nicknamed Sacagawea "Janey." On August 20, 1806, after the expedition had dropped the Charbonneau family at the Knife River villages, he wrote a letter to Charbonneau, which provides insight into his feelings for the family. "You have been a long time with me and have conducted yourself in such a manner as to gain my friendship, your woman who accompanied you that long dangerous and fatiguing route to the Pacific Ocean and back deserved a greater reward for her attention and services on that route than we had in our power to give her." He continued: "As to your little son (my boy Pomp) you well know my fondness for him and my anxiety to take and raise him as my own child." He reiterated his promise to adopt the boy as his son and educate him in St. Louis. He wished the family great success and anxiously awaited a future opportunity to see his "dancing boy Baptiest."

Sacagawea's life after the expedition remains a mystery. An entry for Baptiste in a St. Louis cathedral register dated 1809 records his baptism, but written evidence doesn't offer any more clues about the rest of Sacagawea's life. When did she die? There are various answers. The Hidatsa believe, and the existing written historical record seems to support, that she died at about age twenty-five of putrid fever at Fort Manuel in present-day North Dakota—the source is fur trader John Luttig's journal written in 1812 in which he mentioned that Charbonneau's Snake [Shoshone] wife died. The Lemhi Shoshone accept the Luttig documentation of her death, but the Wind River Shoshone's oral tradition claims she lived to old age with them in Wyoming. Clark made a list of expedition members sometime between 1825 and 1828, and the list indicates that Sacagawea was no longer living.

To address the challenge of telling Sacagawea's story, the exhibition team decided to present the historical evidence and let visitors draw their own conclusions. Which brings us back to August Little Soldier's grand claim and the potential pitfalls of oral tradition. I concluded that perhaps he believes the story he told me of the romance between Sacagawea and Clark, but most Indians I encountered would not. This demonstrates the slippery slope of oral tradition in the historical world. Historians rely on evidence to build an interpretation—or a case. The evidence they often use is the written record, but they also use photographs and artifacts. A fourth source is oral history—often in the format of interviews or transcriptions from interviews. Each source has limitations and, as a trial lawyer knows, the strongest case is built on a combination of sources that corroborate the point. In the Sacagawea story, the oral tradition is far from consistent.

Historians suspicious of oral tradition are sometimes considered insensitive to cultures that did not pass down knowledge and memory through written word. These cultures argue that the strength of the oral tradition is the exacting process. Often one or two people in the tribe were designated "historians" and they carefully collected the tribe's stories and, at a certain time, passed those stories down to the next generation, requiring exact word-for-word repetition. As Carolyn Gilman argues, "Whereas Euro-American society trusts the written record more than the spoken record, the opposite is true in traditional Indian society: what is spoken is trusted, and what is written is suspected of bias."

Many people will continue to tell the story of Sacagawea, both the facts and the myths. Since she couldn't tell her story, all we can do is critically analyze the evidence and draw our own conclusions.

12
A GRIZZLY
IN THE
MAIL

The wonderful power of life which these animals
possess renders them dreadful; their very track
in the mud or sand, which we have sometimes
found 11 inches long and 7¼ inches wide,
exclusive of the talons, is alarming.

—*Meriwether Lewis*

One summer day in St. Louis a large box arrived at the Missouri Historical Society addressed to me. I was gathering a collection of fur
samples to include in the exhibition. We wanted to feature animals
that Lewis and Clark saw for the first time, and we had managed
to secure samples of sea otter, antelope, and coyote. The final hide
on our list was the grizzly bear's. Obtaining a sample proved more
challenging than we had expected because the animal is federally
protected in the lower forty-eight states. Our expert researcher, Jeff,
had spent months searching for a grizzly hide. He finally contacted

the Alaska state game commission, and a staff member promised to send us grizzly fur and a few claws. This delivery from Alaska represented a labor of determination and perseverance, so with great excitement the exhibition team gathered around.

Jeff and I ripped open the box and immediately staggered back, gagging as a pungent stench spread throughout the room. Once recovered but still holding our breath, we carefully unwrapped a plastic bag filled with what appeared to be a whole grizzly skin, paws and claws attached, minus the head. We had expected a tanned hide, but this thing's strong odor made us wonder just how fresh it was. We quickly closed the box and I decided to find a taxidermist who could tan the hide for us. So, under the category "other duties as assigned" I set out to locate a taxidermist, careful to rewrap the stinking package before throwing it in the trunk of my car. The enduring stench would linger many days both in the office and the car.

Having never set foot in a taxidermist shop, I was curious to see what reaction the skin would bring. Not every day someone takes a grizzly bear hide to a taxidermist in the St. Louis area. The man behind the counter directed me to spread the hide on the floor, garnering an instant crowd. A grizzly pelt was a rare thing to the folks in Arnold, Missouri. A part of me wanted to say, "Yep, got a big one here. Found it out in the Ozarks, I did." The taxidermist agreed to the work, and we were pleased with the results.

The exhibition featured a beautiful bear claw necklace. Lewis wrote of the Shoshone, "[B]rave men wear collars made of the claws of the brown bear which are also esteemed of great value and are preserved with great care." The team wanted to give visitors an opportunity to touch a claw, and Jeff volunteered to work on the claws. Jeff stunk up his kitchen first cutting the claws from the fur and then boiling them for hours in water and Borax to clean them. He arrived the next day at work with clean and very sharp grizzly claws, quite proud of his efforts.

Respect the Grizzly

Mandan Indians had warned the men of the Corps that they would encounter fierce bears. Lewis wrote, "The Indians give a very formidable account of the strength and ferocity of this animal." Northern Plains Indians greatly respected the grizzly and hunting the animal was just as much a spiritual experience as it was physical. Elaborate preparation preceded the hunt, including dances and songs to the Bear Spirit. Large hunting parties of up to ten Indians tracked grizzlies. The warrior who successfully killed a bear earned the right to wear a bear claw necklace and received adulation and honor from his tribe. Lewis and Clark had never seen grizzlies before, but were familiar with the smaller and less aggressive black bears of the East. They were confident in their guns and their abilities as hunters, so they could not imagine that the bears would cause them problems. Lewis wrote, "The Indians may well fear this animal . . . but in the hands of skillful riflemen they are by no means as formidable or dangerous as they have been represented." However, he changed his mind after only a few encounters. The size and roar of the animal "staggered the resolution" of the men, he wrote. They quickly learned that they needed up to ten bullets to kill one of the ferocious animals. After several encounters, Lewis concluded, "I find that the curiosity of our party is pretty well satisfied with respect to this animal." Lewis himself began referring to them as "gentlemen."

The exhibition included a section about animal encounters on the expedition, and several stunning artifacts illustrated the perspective of the Northern Plains tribes toward the grizzly. A Western Sioux grizzly bear headdress made from the upper half of a bear's head included the fur-covered upper skull and snout. Once owned by a Teton Lakota man named Bear Head, it eventually came to reside in the collection of the National Museum of Natural History. Headdresses like it were worn in curing ceremonies or in dances held in preparation for a bear hunt. Another item from that collection, one of my favorite artifacts, was a bear shield cover depicting a simple image of a red bear paw with five long claws, with smaller claws drawn around the edge. An animal portrayed on a shield was thought to give its bearer power and protection in battle. Most impressive was the bear claw necklace, another loan from the National Museum of Natural History. It included thirty-five curved four-inch-long claws, worn with the sharp ends next to the bare skin.

Five-Year Scavenger Hunt

We borrowed artifacts for the exhibition from more than fifty institutions around the United States. During what she called a "five-year scavenger hunt," Carolyn and Jeff traveled to museums across the country searching for the perfect objects that would illustrate the story she wanted to tell. And many times they needed to research objects to establish an authentic provenance; in other words, they could not always accept on faith the object's records because overenthusiastic curators and suspect art and antique dealers wanted items to have a Lewis and Clark connection. The objects in the exhibition fell into three main categories: actual artifacts used by key players in the story (such as Lewis's pipe tomahawk), artifacts from the time period like those the corps would have used or seen (such as an air gun or wool socks), and Native artifacts dated as close to the correct time period as possible (such as a side-fold dress). In a subcategory all their own were the objects that traveled on the actual expedition, such as the journals.

It was a major coup that the Missouri Historical Society managed to convince institutions to lend their Lewis and Clark artifacts for the national tour. During the bicentennial, any organization that owned Lewis and Clark artifacts did not want to part with them. A great deal of persuasion was required in some cases to even borrow items for one or two venues on the tour. At times it seemed as if we were dealing with holy relics.

When the expedition returned to St. Louis in September 1806, many items were sold at auction as army surplus, bringing in a grand total of $408.62. No national museum existed and the expedition's prominent place in history was far from secure. The many scientific specimens the corps had collected scattered to various places of science in Philadelphia. Most of the botanic specimens belong to the Academy of Natural Sciences in Philadelphia, the exhibition's second stop. But eleven of the specimens ended up in Kew Gardens, the Royal Botanic Gardens in London. While on a personal trip to London during the research phase, I made a stop at Kew to look at the specimens. Though the Academy of Natural Sciences had more than enough specimens to cover the elaborate rotation schedule we were planning, we wanted to see the condition of the Kew specimens just in case. As I stared at the dried plants taped carefully to the paper, the full emotional power of the objects hit me. Meriwether Lewis had picked these specimens. I couldn't help but marvel at the journey they had taken from the American West to London. Lewis had recruited a young German botanist in Philadelphia to study the plants for a publication. The botanist moved to England for a job and took some of the specimens with him. Eventually the specimens ended up at a Sotheby's auction and made their way to Kew, and it was only in the 1950s that a researcher verified them as a Lewis and Clark specimen.

Carolyn enjoyed the research on the artifacts' provenance just as much as the research about their use. As she wrote in the exhibition catalog, "The process of tracing and authenticating the artifacts that are included required accounting for their chains of provenance— how they were passed down from owner to owner until they came to their present locations. This process revealed that the objects have gone through nearly as many adventures as the Corps of Discovery itself. Their stories are full of lawsuits, eccentric descendants, scholars absconding with the goods, and tragic museum fires."

While I managed to do quite a bit of research about Lewis and Clark, I rarely did object research. On occasion, however, it was all hands on deck and I rolled up my sleeves. On one such occasion, I made a call to the Museum of Comparative Zoology at Harvard requesting to borrow Lewis's woodpecker specimen, a stuffed dead bird that evidence suggests was collected on the expedition. (They agreed to a loan.) And I was adamant that no exhibition about Lewis and Clark would be complete without a full-size standing grizzly, fangs bared and claws outstretched. According to scientist Daniel Botkin, the expedition encountered thirty-seven grizzlies during the westward part of the trip. Our visitors needed to have an encounter as well. Since it was my idea, it became my project. With Jeff's help I located all sizes of stuffed grizzlies on all four feet, not standing as I wanted, and Kodiak brown bears, but since Lewis and Clark had not been in Alaska, they wouldn't work. The bear we finally selected came from the Illinois State Museum. We settled for a smallish grizzly that looked like a teenage bear. It wasn't the ferocious bear I had envisioned, but we included the cast of a ten-inch-long and seven-inch-wide grizzly paw print, which helped visitors imagine the tremendous size of an adult bear. In addition, a segment on the audio tour included ferocious roars. Despite its small frame, the bear, combined with touchable fur and claws, proved extremely popular with visitors of all ages, and I felt satisfied.

The Artifacts Arrive

Fall 2003 began a new phase in our project timeline: case and artifact installation. In my opinion this is the most exciting time in the entire process of exhibition development, when the team's grand vision becomes reality—the concepts that have sprung from deep within the brain become three dimensional. Seeing the cases filled with carefully mounted objects lit brightly (or not so brightly), the large graphic panels, and the newly finished interactives—all the coordinated efforts of a team—brings a deep feeling of accomplishment. I can look at many sets of plans and architectural drawings, but the exhibition never feels "real" until it is built, an amazing jump from paper to reality. In the weeks before an exhibition opens, every day brings new progress.

The months preceding the opening felt like Christmas as objects arrived almost daily from museums and archive collections across the country. The team had been studying images of the objects for years and we were thrilled to finally see them in person. The air gun arrived from the Milwaukee Public Museum, Lewis's pipe tomahawk arrived from the Alabama Department of Archives and History, and Lewis's Masonic apron arrived amid controversy from Montana (there was a faction that did not want it to leave the state and the story made headlines). Plant specimens arrived from Philadelphia, the calumet pipe from Boston, the compass from the Smithsonian, Lewis's branding iron from Portland, the elk antlers from Monticello—and the list continued. While my responsibility did not include the actual installation of the objects, I managed to sneak peeks at the staging area on a regular basis.

Friends always asked me if I had a favorite artifact, but this was an impossible question to answer. Carolyn identified a series of "not-to-miss" artifacts we called "the treasures" that were mounted in special stand-alone cases prominently located in a central path through the exhibition. These objects would lure visitors from section to section and included Lewis's Masonic apron, Jefferson's theodolite (a surveying tool), the elk skin journal, and a Northern Plains Indian side-fold dress. Another item was Lewis's pipe tomahawk. The stem of the exquisite piece was crafted of polished maple, with a thin squiggly sliver inlay of silver down the length. Handed down in the family for generations, the pipe was probably the one Lewis had with him at his death in 1809, though Carolyn was not able to verify whether Lewis took it on the expedition. I was fascinated with the pipe and counted it among my favorite artifacts.

World of Women

Another item, quite ordinary and similar to one taken on the expedition was a corn mill, a hand-cranked iron and wood tool used to grind corn. The story we told with this artifact proved very popular and became my favorite lesson in the teacher curriculum. President Jefferson had written to Lewis requesting that he take along several of the mills to give the Indians to teach them agricultural practices. The corn was poured into a metal funnel and ground with the turn of a crank, which made the process of producing meal much less tedious. Lewis had purchased several of the mills in Philadelphia. When they reached the Mandan tribes, the men noted in the journals that they had presented the chiefs with a mill. Clark wrote the gift was "very thankfully received." Other Corps members recorded that "they appeared delighted with the steel mill" and "those people appeared much pleased with the corn mill." However, almost two years later, a North West Company fur trader named Alexander Henry was passing through the same village and wrote in his journal that he "saw the remains of an excellent large corn mill which the foolish fellows had demolished to barb their arrows; the largest piece of it, which they could not break up or work up into any weapon, was fixed to a wooden handle, and used to pound marrowbones to make grease." What happened? In what Carolyn described as a cultural misinterpretation, Lewis and Clark had presented the gifts to the wrong people. In Mandan culture, it was the women who grew the crops and processed the corn. The women controlled the food supply and if a man wanted to eat, he was dependent on the women. The Mandan men did not undertake the tiring labor of grinding the corn with a mortar and pestle and thus did not understand the mill's value as a tool. They only saw its value in the materials it was made from, so they cut it up to use for weapons. A mill borrowed from the Colonial Williamsburg Foundation collection allowed us to tell this story in the exhibition.

Speaking of Indian women, the men of the corps were enamored with Native women and knowing his men, Lewis had prepared for the inevitable. The artifact that proved the most memorable to my friends was only eight inches long. It both repelled and intrigued them—having seen it on display in St. Louis, my friends Jon and Paul joined me on a trip to Denver and saw the exhibition again there. The first artifact they set out to find was the urethral syringe, or as Lewis called them on his list of supplies, four "pewter penis syringes." Lewis brought along the standard remedies for venereal disease and began treating the men in January 1805. When the disease caused urinary blockage, out came the syringe to irrigate the urethra. Borrowed from the Mutter Museum in Philadelphia, the syringe never ceased to send chills down the spine of male visitors.

The document I most identified with was a letter Lewis wrote to his mother, Lucy Marks, prior to leaving for the expedition. The poignant letter, a private message from son to mother, sought to calm a mother's fear, assure her of his safety, assuage his guilt at not having an opportunity for one last visit, and give directions for financial matters. As the oldest son in a family of five children, Lewis held great responsibility. Marks was a widow by that point, and Lewis had inherited the family estate when he turned twenty-one. Unfortunately there are no known letters from Marks to Lewis. The only other letter between them related to the expedition is one written from Fort Mandan during the first winter of the expedition. Lewis tells his mother about the challenges of navigating the Missouri, of the friendly Mandan neighbors, and of the scenery. Sadly, though he must have written a triumphant letter to his mother upon his return to St. Louis at the end of the expedition, no letter survives. A letter he wrote to President Jefferson on the day he arrived ends with a personal note: "I am very anxious to learn the state of my friends in Albemarle [VA] particularly whether my mother is yet living." Little did he know that she would outlive him by twenty-eight years.

Opening Day

"Lewis & Clark: The National Bicentennial Exhibition" opened with great fanfare in St. Louis in January 2004. A parade of Indian nations in full regalia of all colors marched through the grand atrium at the Missouri History Museum. A fife and drum corps followed, along with an honor guard of Lewis and Clark reenactors. We exhibition team members were honored by the presence of many of our Indian friends and advisers from around the country. It signified that we had accomplished Carolyn Gilman's vision—to tell the story of the cultural landscape with sensitivity and detailed complexity.

During the years of the bicentennial, 2004–2006, a great deal of national attention focused on the anniversary. The exhibition traveled across the country and hundreds of thousands of people came to see the unique collection of artifacts. The U.S. Postal Service printed stamps in honor of the expedition and the U.S. Mint struck nickels honoring the Corps of Discovery. The National Park Service developed a traveling interpretive exhibit, and a series of signature events organized by the National Lewis and Clark Bicentennial Council took place all along the expedition's trail from Monticello in Virginia to Portland, Oregon. Each focused on a different aspect of the journey, and each one included a Native perspective. Communities dedicated new monuments to the explorers, publishers printed numerous new books about the expedition, and travel publications featured many articles on the events.

Woven through all the commemoration was the desire to find new understanding of this saga familiar to so many Americans. Those of us on the presenting side also hoped to correct misconceptions related to the expedition. Several had always bothered me. One of the biggest misconceptions is that the expedition was a result of the Louisiana Purchase. Having purchased this vast tract of land, President Jefferson sent Lewis and Clark to find out what he bought. The reality is that Jefferson had planned the expedition before the purchase took place. Lewis and Clark were expecting to travel through foreign territory and President Jefferson had gone through diplomatic channels to secure proper permissions. Another misconception has to do with Sacagawea and York, Clark's slave. Though a great deal has been written about them, the truth is that historians don't know much about either Sacagawea's or York's story. And although many people think that there was only one fatality on the expedition (Sgt. Charles Floyd succumbed to peritonitis resulting from an infected appendix and was buried with military honors on a river bluff they named for him), the truth is that at least two Blackfoot Indians were killed in a confrontation with Lewis and several of his men on the return trip. The expedition members, separated from the main party, had unexpectedly encountered several young Blackfeet and shared a camp site one night. Lewis awoke in the morning to shouts. The Blackfeet were stealing their guns and horses and Lewis was determined to stop the thefts. He shot one Indian and in the confusion, one of the expedition members stabbed another. The Blackfeet, as was their custom, were attempting to gain honor in the tribe by proving contact with the enemies. Lewis described the event in detail in his journal, but the incident often gets left out of the narrative.

After eight months on display in St. Louis, the exhibition closed in September of 2004 and moved on to the next venue, Philadelphia. It had been a whirlwind period of docent training, school programs, special events, and electronic field trips. Now, my work was finished and my job in St. Louis officially came to an end. My colleague Jeff continued to travel with the exhibition, ensuring proper installation and care of the artifacts. My involvement continued briefly as a contractor in Philadelphia, where I trained the volunteers and staff at the Academy of Natural Sciences. However, at that point I began to consider life beyond Lewis and Clark. I had gotten to know them quite well over three years and was ready to move on.

Gifts to Remember

Two years later, in the fall of 2006, my Lewis and Clark journey came to a symbolic end. The exhibition's national tour made its final stop in Washington DC. My colleague and friend Jeff sent an e-mail asking for my address. He had deinstalled the exhibition and wanted to send me a memento. My mind reviewed the various reproduction objects we had acquired. What would he send? When the small but heavy package arrived, I had my answer: a Jefferson peace medal and a small white ermine skin, whiskers and all. Very appropriate, I thought, and symbolic. They represented gifts exchanged on the expedition—medals from Lewis and Clark to the Indian chiefs and the ermine skin from a Shoshone chief to Meriwether Lewis.

President Jefferson charged Lewis and Clark with opening diplomatic relations with a variety of Indian nations whose cultures were unfamiliar to Americans. The captains utilized a number of strategies to accomplish this, one being the presentation of peace medals as symbols of friendship and alliance. The practice of presenting medals to Indians did not originate with the United States. The French, British, and Spanish had distributed medals for many decades prior to the Lewis and Clark expedition. The medals Lewis and Clark carried came in five sizes, to designate five "ranks" of chief. Such hierarchy reflected their own social system more than the Indians'. There were three sizes of medals featuring Jefferson's profile. The reverse side featured two hands clasped in greeting and a crossed tomahawk and pipe. When they distributed the medals, often with grand ceremony, Lewis and Clark usually had no way of knowing a correct leadership hierarchy, which constantly shifted. They were essentially "making chiefs," as they called it. On August 3, 1804, Clark wrote that he "made up a small present for those people in proportion to their consequence, also a package with a medal to accompany a speech for the Grand Chief. . . . after hearing what they had to say, delivered a medal of second grade . . . one for the Ottos and one for the Missouri and presented 4 medals of a third grade to the inferior chiefs two for each tribe."

Consider the symbols on the medals. What might clasped hands convey to tribes that didn't shake hands in greeting? The tribes they met on the upper Missouri had not had contact with Europeans. Trader Francois La Rocque wrote about meeting a Crow chief in 1805: "When we offered to shake hands with this great man, he did not understand the intention, and stood motionless until he was informed that shaking hands was the sign of friendship among white men." The Shoshone did not shake hands, but surprised Lewis with great affection. Lewis described it this way: "These men then advanced and embraced me very affectionately in their way which is by putting their left arm over your right shoulder clasping your back, while they apply their left cheek to yours and frequently vociferate the word ah-hi-e, ah-hi-e that is, I am much pleased, I am much rejoiced. Both parties now advanced and we were all caressed and besmeared with their grease and paint till I was heartily tired of the national hug."

What did Jefferson's portrait mean to a tribe in the Bitterroot Mountains? Lewis and Clark found themselves in a complicated and political world that was difficult to understand. Tribes on the lower Missouri River had different expectations than those on the upper Missouri. The tribes they met each had different experiences with European contact, and some had none at all. Lewis and Clark couldn't begin to understand the complex layers of alliances and enemies that existed between the tribes.

When Lewis and Clark met up with the Shoshone Indians in what is now Montana, they were desperate for horses to cross the Bitterroot Mountains. Lewis had arrived days before Clark and the rest of the party, and the Shoshone were nervous. They had been running from the Blackfeet and were fearful that Lewis's party was a trap. Lewis had to convince the Shoshone leader to stay until Clark appeared. In a moment of great uncertainty, Cameahwait offered a gesture of trust. Lewis wrote, "The chief with much ceremony put tippets about our necks such as they themselves wore. To give them further confidence I put my cocked hat with feather on the chief." Carolyn was convinced that at this moment Lewis came the closest he ever would to understanding the Indian world. The exhibition's central film documented this moment and its importance to the expedition and in Lewis's life. Lewis treasured his tippet (or mantle) made of otter skins and 140 ermine skins and presented it to Peale's Museum in Philadelphia upon his return.

My Journey of Discovery

The Lewis and Clark expedition was a journey of discovery on many levels. And so was my Lewis and Clark journey. Like the men of the expedition, I, too, had crossed cultural divides. I stepped into Indian worlds and glimpsed briefly the state of tribal cultures today.

At Salish Kootenai College on the Flathead Indian Reservation at the foot of the Mission Mountains in western Montana, I led a group of reservation teachers in a primary source activity focused on documents. Some of the group stated that American history as written today is selective and slanted toward a white male mythology. They wanted to talk about oral traditions and shared some with the group. A member of the Salish tribe told us that the Lewis and Clark expedition was a business trip for the United States, meant to catalog resources to expand a trading empire. Another said that most people aren't aware that transcontinental travel was not a new concept for Indians and that many tribes were part of vast and complex trade networks.

I spent the evening in a school gym at Two Eagle River School in Pablo, Montana, attending a cross-cultural music and dance performance and workshop. The night began with a small group of Indian youths gathered around a large drum. They began a steady beating and raised their voices in high-pitched intense singing. To my ears, it sounded like wailing and I found its musical patterns hard to understand. It didn't seem to follow any Western rules. Members of the Salish tribe graciously demonstrated several dances and then called my group to join them. Not confident in my dancing abilities, I reluctantly walked onto the dance floor. We started with a circle dance, followed by an owl dance and a home sweet home dance. We learned to rhythmically follow the drumbeats, standing on the ball of one foot, heel raised then lowered, and then switching to the opposite foot.

Next an Irish fiddle group performed and the group danced a few contra dances popular in eighteenth- and nineteenth-century America. The driving melody of the violins was a strong contrast to the drums and the dances seemed worlds apart. This exchange of music and dance again prompted us to think of the cultural exchanges on the Lewis and Clark expedition. The corps took two violins on the journey and many journal entries record the exchange of music with Native tribes. Clark wrote that "Peter Cruzatte [the party's principal fiddler] played on the violin and the men danced which delighted the natives." Lewis mentioned that "some of the men danced; after which the natives entertained us with a dance after their method." John Ordway noted that members of the expedition "danced among them and they were much pleased, and said they would dance day and night until we return." A two-day visit with the Walla Walla tribe on the return trip ended with a dance—"The Wallah Wallahs . . . formed a half circle around our camp where they waited very patiently to see our party dance. The fiddle was played and the men amused themselves with dancing about an hour. We then requested the Indians to dance . . . the whole assemblage of Indians about 350 men, women, and children sang and danced at the same time."

My work on the Lewis and Clark exhibition taught me a great deal about perspectives and changing interpretations. Who knows if there will be an exhibition in 2104 to mark the tricentennial. What interpretive approach might it take? The basic facts don't change, but what new historical evidence might be uncovered? During the development of the exhibition, a number of letters written by William Clark to his brother Jonathan were published for the first time. They provided new insight into Clark's feelings about his slave, York, and allowed us to tell more of York's story. Historian Eric Foner has written that "[h]istory always has been and always will be regularly rewritten, in response to new questions, new information, new methodologies, and new political, social, and cultural imperatives." This fact is often difficult for nonhistorians to accept, even though most realize there are many ways to recount past events. The historians of the future will no doubt find new interpretations of the Lewis and Clark story and, who knows, maybe somewhere there is a record of Sacagawea's dying words or a buffalo hide painting that provides new insight into a tribe's encounters with the explorers . . .

13
TRACKING
THE
BUFFALO

It not only took a skillful man, but a brave
one, to face a herd of buffalo with nothing
but a trusty bow and a quiver full of arrows.

—*Luther Standing Bear, Lakota*

The bison, like the bald eagle, holds an iconic place in the American
psyche and its story is one of near extinction and rebirth. The American bison, commonly called the buffalo though unrelated to both
the African and Asian buffalo, once roamed large areas of the North
American continent but gradually came to represent one region: the
American West. Many of the early Western explorers like Lewis and
Clark were awestruck by the huge herds they encountered. Captain
John C. Fremont of the U.S. Corps of Topographical Engineers led
an expedition in 1842 to map the area between the Missouri River
and the Rocky Mountains. On July 4 he wrote, "As we were riding
slowly along this afternoon, clouds of dust in the ravines among the

hills to the right suddenly attracted our attention, and in a few minutes column after column of buffalo came galloping down, making directly for the river. By the time the leading herds had reached the water, the prairie was darkened with the dense masses . . . from hill to hill the prairie bottom was certainly not less than two miles wide; and, allowing the animals to be ten feet apart, and only ten in a line, there were already eleven thousand in view. Some idea may thus be formed of their number when they had occupied the whole plain. In a short time they surrounded us on every side; extending for several miles in the rear and forward as far as the eye could reach."

A Hide Painting with a Story

My fascination with buffalo started with a hide painting at the National Museum of American History. One of the Hands On History Room activities featured a contemporary buffalo hide painting by the Three Affiliated Tribes (Mandan, Hidatsa, and Arikara) artist Dennis Fox. The HOHR's developers had commissioned the artwork especially for the space to teach visitors about the history of buffalo in the American West using a traditional storytelling technique. Plains Indians painted on dried hides for reasons both practical and symbolic. Sometimes tribal elders painted a winter count design, which kept a record of the tribe's history, a different symbol representing each year. Or a woman might paint a geometric pattern to hasten childbearing or a man might paint a battle scene to memorialize a mighty victory.

Lewis and Clark saw many examples of painted hides on their expedition. In the spring of 1805 they sent a big package, including seven buffalo robes, to President Jefferson. One painted hide depicted a battle between the Mandan and Hidatsa versus the Arikara and Sioux and had been a gift to the explorers. Jefferson displayed it in the entrance hall of his home Monticello for years, and during the bicentennial of the expedition the staff at Monticello hired Dennis Fox to create a similar robe (the original hide given to Jefferson has been lost).

The colorful hide Mr. Fox painted for the Hands On History Room did not depict tribal warfare but told a different story. In fact it told many stories, both spiritual and historical, about the buffalo and the place of honor the buffalo holds in Plains Indians' culture. The museum visitor's job was to decipher the stories. At the top left of the hide, a buffalo emerged from a cave beneath the Little Missouri River in South Dakota. Once a water animal, the buffalo was trapped on land when the river suddenly froze, becoming a land animal. A painted buffalo skull at the top center of the painting indicated the direction "north," the place many late-nineteenth-century Indians thought the buffalo herds had disappeared to. Nine rare white buffalo hides in a circle in the middle signified the great number of buffalo that once existed.

The hide also told the tragic story of cultures that relied on the buffalo for life and a culture that slaughtered buffalo for commercial gain. On either side of the painting, a herd of twenty-two buffalo run from eight hunters, four on foot and four on horseback, carrying bows and arrows. One buffalo lay dead on each side, with red at its stomach and a knife nearby—portraying the fact that the Indians took only the buffalo they needed and often used almost all parts of the animal. In contrast, below were ten dead buffalo shot by two hunters. There is blood coming out of their mouths, signifying the fact that many commercial hunters killed only for the hide and the tongue, a delicacy. They left the rest to rot.

Below the ten dead buffalo, Fox had painted a fence and about sixty cattle—signifying the transformation of the land to ranching. A locomotive on one side and wagon train on the other, with masses of non-Indians portrayed at the bottom of the hide, completed the story, signifying the end of a wild land and a way of life.

Dark Days for the Buffalo

In the late 1990s, the staff decided to experiment with adapting several of the activities in the Hands On History Room to the Web medium. While I had not been involved with developing the original hide activity, I jumped at the opportunity to experiment with this new technology. Since the hide painting activity was strongly visual in format, we thought it might be easier to adapt. As we researched and wrote the Web activity, it changed greatly from the physical activity. The Web allowed for a layered approach and the final product, "Tracking the Buffalo, Stories from a Buffalo Hide Painting," offered much more historical context than the original activity. It allowed us to give users access to a variety of historical sources. I thought the final product turned out to be more successful than the original history room activity.

As we developed the Web site, we looked for other pieces of evidence to support and supplement the story of the buffalo. We wanted to give people the opportunity to review the evidence and draw their own conclusions. The photos we found were startling. A print from *Frank Leslie's Illustrated Newspaper* in 1871 showed white men with rifles shooting at a herd of buffalo from a train on the Kansas-Pacific Railroad. Another photo showed men posing in front of the railroad's office with about twenty-five mounted buffalo heads piled around them. A photo from Dodge City in 1874 showed a man sitting on a huge pile of buffalo hides.

The 1870s became a decade defined as the great slaughter of buffalo. Buffalo hides were worth big money. At a time when the average day laborer earned around $1 a day, a good buffalo hide could bring between $3 and $50. Frank H. Mayer, a twenty-two-year-old former Confederate bugler, was looking for adventure when he ran into two buffalo hunters who encouraged him to head for the Plains. "The buffalo didn't belong to anybody. If you could kill them, what they brought was yours. They were walking gold pieces." Hides and tongues were shipped east by the thousands. In its first three months of existence, the town of Dodge City, Kansas, shipped 43,029 hides to the urban centers of the East. Across western Kansas, an estimated 1.5–3 million buffalo were killed in just over two years.

That the extermination of the buffalo greatly impacted the Plains

Indian cultures was obvious to all. The Texas legislature was considering outlawing poaching on tribal lands and General Philip Sheridan, famous leader during the Civil War and later the Indian Wars, purportedly testified against legislation: "These men [buffalo hunters] have done more in the last two years, and will do in the next year, more to settle the vexed Indian question than the entire regular Army has done in the last thirty years. They are destroying the Indians' commissary; it is well known that an army losing its base of supplies is placed at a great disadvantage. For the sake of lasting peace, let them kill, skin, and sell until the buffaloes are exterminated. Then your prairies can be covered with speckled cattle and festive cowboy, who follows the hunter as a second forerunner of an advanced civilization."

Old Lady Horse, from the Kiowa culture, offered a different perspective: "Everything the Kiowas had came from the buffalo. . . . The buffalo were the life of the Kiowa. . . . The buffalo loved their people as much as the Kiowas loved them. . . . So when the white man wanted to build railroads, or when they wanted to farm and raise cattle, the buffalo protected the Kiowa. They tore up the railroad tracks and the gardens. They chased the cattle off the ranges. Then the white man hired hunters to do nothing but kill the buffalo. Up and down the plain these men ranged, shooting sometimes as many as a hundred buffalo a day. Behind them came skinners with their wagons. They piled the hides . . . into the wagons until they were full and then took their loads to the new railroad stations that were being built, to be shipped east to the market."

Buffalo hunter Frank Mayer later reflected on his role in the demise of the buffalo: "We runners [hunters] served our purpose in helping abolish the buffalo; maybe it was our ruthless harvesting of him which telescoped the control of the Indian by a decade or maybe more. Or maybe I am just rationalizing. Maybe we were just a greedy lot who wanted to get ours, and to hell with posterity, the buffalo, or anyone else, just so we kept our scalps on and our money pouches filled. I think maybe that is the way it was."

During additional research I came across a painting called *American Progress*, painted by John Gast in 1872. It featured many of the same symbols that were on the museum's buffalo hide and serves as an allegory of American triumphalism, the idea that it was the American nation's destiny to settle the continent from Atlantic to Pacific Ocean and that civilization would triumph over primitivism. The contrast is striking. At the painting's center, a large white-robed woman portraying America faces westward, the cities of the East a haze on one horizon. At her feet a stagecoach carries settlers west. Several railroads are scattered over the landscape. The foreground features farmers behind a plow and oxen, a homestead, and some miners. In front of her, to the west, a band of Indians are driven away, turning in the face of her power. A herd of buffalo run off the edge. She carries a book to represent enlightenment in her right arm and her left hand carries a coil of wire, stringing a line of telegraph poles to bring civilization from the east (ironically, the poles were supposedly difficult to keep standing upright because buffalo often used them as scratching posts, destroying them). This juxtaposition of the two paintings, so different in style but similar in symbolism, served as a wonderful teaching opportunity.

The museum's buffalo hide painting was a strong visual display but did not work for the visitors who wanted to touch. After a search, I found the perfect object. If there's one thing that is guaranteed to capture the attention of any students, elementary through high school, it is a dried buffalo bladder. It looks like a crackly blown-up balloon and when moistened can serve as a canteen. Put it inside a rectangular box made of buffalo hide, fur on the outside, and you have a definite crowd pleaser. The roughly fourteen-by-ten-by-ten-inch furry box held various buffalo parts and items made from buffalo parts, including a spoon molded from buffalo horn, a fly swatter made from a buffalo tail, a small oblong bladder pouch holding porcupine quills, teeth, a rattle made of hoof pieces, and small porous bones used as a paint brush. Unfortunately we weren't able to find a buffalo rib sled, popular with Plains Indian children.

I used the buffalo box in the Hands On History Room and later in St. Louis with the Lewis and Clark exhibition, and it proved to be an educational treasure box that never ceased to enthrall visitors. The boxes were produced by the Intertribal Bison Cooperative and supported their educational interests.

Buffalo at the Castle

Many people don't know that in the late 1880s, visitors to Washington's National Museum could view buffalo grazing in a yard behind the Smithsonian Castle. William Temple Hornaday, a taxidermist employed by the museum, collected several animals out west to serve as living models for the taxidermists who prepared exhibits. It was widely believed that buffalo would soon be extinct due to hunting. Hornaday's goal in part was to educate people about buffalo and foster an interest in environmental conservation. In 1887 several thousand people a day visited the buffalo and this popularity led to the birth of another well-loved Washington institution. In 1889 President Cleveland signed a bill establishing the National Zoo, a unit of the Smithsonian. Unfortunately, today the zoo does not keep any buffalo.

During my work on the Web activity, I became quite fond of "buffies," as one of the curators called them. I agree with writer Padgett Powell who said, "I like them because they seem gently wild, as opposed to violently wild, and they have the huge rump-like hump, the giant head, the eyeball the size of a billiard ball. What is not to like?" Like those tourists to Washington in the 1880s, I, too, wanted to see buffalo.

My Buffalo Hunt

When my travels to the West began, I set a goal to see buffalo in the wild. This is not easy to achieve. Today, a visitor to the West must know where to look. A number of state and federally owned herds dot the landscape. On my first trip to Montana, I naively searched vast horizons in vain trying to spot at least one buffalo. As I ventured West for three Lewis and Clark trips, I continued to seek out places where wild buffalo roam. I encountered my first buffalo in a place where many others have had the experience: Yellowstone National Park. The Yellowstone herd, which numbers over three thousand, is the only continuously wild herd in the United States. I had driven around in the park for hours without seeing any buffalo. Then I rounded a bend and saw a sea of cars parked alongside the road. Traffic came to a halt, drivers and passengers eagerly watching five buffalo near the side of the road. I watched in astonishment as judgment went out the window and photographers attempted to get close to the huge wild animals.

This was not the magical buffalo experience I was hoping for. I didn't want to share my experience with a mass of camera-crazed tourists. So while in Montana, I attempted to visit the National Bison Range, one of the oldest wildlife refuges in the country, established in 1908, but it was closed due to wildfires in the area.

Finally, a trip to Utah a year later brought my buffalo dreams to life. Antelope Island, the largest island in the Great Salt Lake, is linked by a narrow causeway to the mainland. Since 1981 the entire island, about the size of the District of Columbia, has been a state park. The arid and barren windswept landscape is a hiker's paradise and its otherworldly topography conjures comparisons to lunar landforms. On a winter ski trip to the Salt Lake City area, I convinced my buddy Jon to visit Antelope Island. Besides wanting to rest my weary muscles after days of skiing, I secretly hoped to get a glimpse of what the American West might have looked like before settlement. I had read that Antelope Island State Park is home to one of the largest publicly owned buffalo herds in the world, averaging over five hundred animals. The herd dates to 1893, when the island's owner managed to transport twelve bison to the island. The herd is one of the oldest in the country and possesses unique genetic characteristics. Careful management has allowed the herd to thrive and an annual roundup takes place each October. Horsemen and helicopters drive the herd to corrals on the northern part of the island where veterinarians check each animal's health and update vaccinations. To control the population, excess animals are sold at auction and shipped off the island.

As we drove along the desolate park roads, I kept my eyes peeled for dark shapes with humps. Finally we came upon several buffies grazing contentedly in a field. It was a memorable scene—low mountains surrounding us, the Great Salt Lake melting into a haze on the horizon, a landscape devoid of the trappings of civilization, with shaggy buffalo contentedly munching on grass—my magical moment at last.

Max Harward lived on a ranch on the island from age nine to twenty-one. He wrote of the excitement and isolation in a book titled *Where the Buffalo Roam: Life on Antelope Island*. He described buffalo hunts and several run-ins with the island's iconic animals: "I have learned to respect this magnificent animal for its strength and determination for independence. Many people learn the hard way that the buffalo will give a warning if they feel threatened and if not heeded, they will defend themselves and their calves until death, if necessary. The illusion of being slow and awkward is quickly gone when you observe them attain top speed from a complete stand-still in just a few jumps."

On one occasion, Harward's friend was charged by a buffalo because his dog had run after it. The only place of safety was under a wagon where he and the dog cowered while the buffalo tried most of the afternoon to rout them out. It finally lost interest and went away.

Buffalo Jumping over Cliffs

I remembered Meriwether Lewis, too, had experienced a charging buffalo. A large buffalo bull swam across the river by the expedition's camp one night. Confused, the animal ran at full speed toward the campfires, within inches of the sleeping men's heads. Lewis credited his dog, Seaman, with saving him as the dog barked and the buffalo changed its course away from Lewis's tent.

Later in that same journal entry, Lewis wrote of passing "the remains of a vast many mangled carcasses of buffalo which had been driven over a precipice of 120 feet by the Indians and perished." He estimated the pile to be at least one hundred carcasses, creating a "most horrid stench." Lewis may have been describing a small buffalo jump.

My first trip to Montana included a visit to one of hundreds of buffalo jumps scattered across the West, mostly in the northern Great Plains. There are over three hundred sites in Montana alone. The Ulm Pishkun buffalo jump stands ten miles southwest of Great Falls, Montana. The Blackfoot term for buffalo jump is *pishkun*, loosely translated as "deep blood kettle." Before the introduction of horses, Plains tribes used high cliffs to kill buffalo. The fifty-foot-high cliffs stretch for a mile in the wide open country. According to officials there, the soil beneath the cliffs is about thirteen feet deep with compacted buffalo bones collected between 900 and 1,500 AD. Meriwether Lewis described the process in his journal: "One of the most active and fleet young men is selected and disguised in a robe of buffalo skin . . . he places himself at a distance between a herd of buffalo and a precipice proper for the purpose; the other Indians now surround the herd on the back and flanks and at a signal agreed on all show themselves at the same time moving forward towards the buffalo; the disguised Indian or decoy has taken care to place himself sufficiently near the buffalo to be noticed by them when they take to flight and running before them they follow him in full speed to the precipice; the Indian (decoy) in the meantime has taken care to secure himself in some cranny in the cliff . . . the part of the decoy I am informed is extremely dangerous."

My colleague Bill teaches courses about Montana history and often takes students to visit buffalo jumps. He challenges them to see the landscape as a tool for human use and they look for signs of how humans have shaped the land. Sometimes he takes students to two different jumps and asks them to compare. They look at the gathering basin (huge natural grazing area where the herd congregated to feed), the drive lanes (where the buffalo were funneled to the cliff), and the campsites and processing areas near the base of the cliff. At some sites small rock cairns still mark the edges of the drive lanes, sometimes many miles from the cliff. These helped steer the buffalo to the cliff. Standing at the top of Ulm Pishkun, I tried to imagine the huge clump of fur and hooves of several hundred buffalo suspended for a split-second in mid-air—for some reason Wile E. Coyote kept coming to mind, frantically running in mid-air as he is propelled off yet another cliff. It's slightly humorous, probably because it's impossible to imagine. When you consider the sound of buffalo bodies bouncing down the cliff sides and bones cracking and the bleating calves looking for their mothers, combined with the stench of death, the humor is gone.

Two Perspectives on the Hunt

While working on the Lewis and Clark exhibition I began to understand the very different relationship that Plains Indians cultivated with animals. To them the animal world was a web of relationships and hunting was about communicating with the spirit of the animal. As Carolyn Gilman put it, "Plains Indians did not believe hunting was a mark of human superiority over animals . . . it was a mark of animal generosity. No animal could be killed unless it consented to give its life graciously so that humans could survive. Before setting out, a hunter would address the animal in prayer with a respectful and humble tone, explaining that he and his family were needy and deserving. When the animal presented itself to be killed, the hunter expressed thanks by treating the animal's body with respect and by giving offerings. European hunters relied on technology; Indian hunters relied on persuasion."

Some members of the Lewis and Clark expedition observed various rituals related to the buffalo hunt and assumed the Indians worshipped the buffalo. Carolyn explained that it was more the spirit that was honored. Takes the Gun, a Lakota born in the nineteenth century, offered this explanation: "The spirit of Tatanka [buffalo] cares for the family. It cares for the little children. It cares for the hunters. It cares for the growing things . . . it cares for everything that has young."

I remember reading about how thrilled Teddy Roosevelt was when he finally shot a buffalo for the first time in North Dakota in the summer of 1883. His hunting guide, Joe Ferris, described it later: "I never saw anyone so enthused in my life. He was so eager to shoot his first buffalo that it somehow got into my blood; and I wanted to see him kill his first one as badly as he wanted to kill it." Roosevelt scrawled an excited note to his wife: "The luck has turned at last. I will bring you home the head of a great buffalo bull." Roosevelt thrilled to the challenge of tracking and matching wits with animals.

Only seven years before Roosevelt's experience, Luther Standing Bear, a Sioux, wrote an eloquent account of his first buffalo hunt as an eight-year-old. He and Roosevelt may have shared the same amount of enthusiasm, but that's where the comparison ends. "It was an event for which every Sioux boy eagerly waited. To ride side by side with the best hunters of the tribe, to hear the terrible noise of the great herds as they ran, and then to help bring home the kill was the most thrilling day of any Indian boy's life." He described the hunt: "The herd was now running and had raised a cloud of dust. I felt no fear until we had entered this cloud of dust and I could see nothing about me—only hear the sound of feet . . . I was in the midst of the buffalo, their dark bodies rushing all about me and their great heads moving up and down to the sound of their hoofs beating upon the earth. I was seized by blank fear." Standing Bear ended up finding a young calf, just the size he could manage. He killed it with five arrows, wryly noting that a good hunter would have used just one. He briefly considered lying to his father about the number of arrows he used, but ultimately told the truth. When he described the memory years later in 1931, Standing Bear said, "I felt more glad than ever that I had told the truth and I have never regretted it. I am more proud now that I told the truth than I am of killing the buffalo." This hunt in about 1876 would be his first and last buffalo hunt. "It lives only in my memory, for the days of the buffalo are over."

Though a way of life based on the bison ended, the animal did not disappear. Through the efforts of organizations like the Intertribal Bison Cooperative (ITBC), the buffalo is slowly making a comeback on tribal lands. While working on the Lewis and Clark exhibition Web site, I had the opportunity to interview Fred DuBray, a member of the Cheyenne River Sioux tribe in South Dakota, and founder and first president of ITBC. The cooperative was formed in 1990 to help tribes return the buffalo to Indian Country. DuBray explained the council's mission: "To reestablish healthy buffalo populations on tribal lands is to reestablish hope for Indian people. Reintroduction of the buffalo to tribal lands will help heal the spirit of both the Indian people and the buffalo." Today the ITBC boasts a membership of over fifty-seven tribes and its collective herd numbers over fifteen thousand bison on tribal lands. DuBray told me that "as we restore our buffalo herds back to health, we will also begin to restore our people back to health."

An Award of Distinction

When I left the National Museum of American History to move to St. Louis, my coworkers presented me with a humorous "award." The citation featured a detail of one of the photos we had used in the buffalo hide painting online activity. It's a photo of a man wearing what appear to be his Sunday clothes: white shirt, tie, coat, pocket handkerchief, watch chain dangling at his waist. He stands with one hand on his hip and a hat cocked on his head, in front of a Kansas Pacific Railroad office, surrounded by a shocking collection of mounted buffalo heads prepared by the railroad's taxidermist. An image of my face had been photoshopped onto the man. The inscription read: "The Buffalo Hunter Award, presented to Tim Grove for his perseverance in pursuing provocative presentations of primary sources in pedagogic service to the American people."

14
THE CATHEDRAL AND THE CEMETERY

When these acorns that are falling
At our feet are oaks overshadowing
Our children in a remote century, this
mute green bank will be full of history

—*Ralph Waldo Emerson at the consecration*
of Sleepy Hollow Cemetery

Looking back on that colorless December day, I wonder what it was that pulled me to Bellefontaine Cemetery in St. Louis. The Lewis and Clark exhibition was moving on, and so was I. My three-year job had ended and my search for a new position had begun in earnest. The East Coast beckoned me to return to the familiar. I had traveled to Philadelphia several times that fall to train staff at the exhibition's next venue, the Academy of Natural Sciences. I was doing what I could to help ensure the exhibition's success in Philadelphia. But the dreary day that I visited the cemetery was decision day—a job offer was on the table and my thoughts weighed me down. I ended up visiting two places that had brought me serenity during my years in St. Louis: the cemetery and, before that, a cathedral.

History in Churches

The Cathedral Basilica of St. Louis, a huge green-domed, two-towered Romanesque structure, sits on Lindell Boulevard west of downtown. Inside its massive oak doors eighty-three thousand feet of brightly colored mosaics draw the eyes upward. Whereas some cathedrals tell stories in their stained glass windows, this cathedral uses tiles. It boasts one of the world's largest collections of mosaics. Every dome, soffit, arch, pendentive, and lunette is covered with glass tiles or tesserae of over seven thousand colors.

Here approximately 41.5 million brilliant tiles tell stories from the history of the Catholic Church in America and in St. Louis, along with stories of the Christian faith. Gazing up, a visitor sees images of America's saints and martyrs, milestones in the Catholic Church's presence in St. Louis, and the early frontier mission activities of fathers Jacques Marquette and Pierre-Jean De Smet. The story of the desegregation of the city's parochial schools sits alongside the blue seal of the city of St. Louis, with its Mississippi River steamboat.

The mosaics and gleaming marble floors and columns of the cathedral never ceased to lift my spirits and encouraged me to ponder higher callings. So I returned for perhaps one last visit to the place that had served as a spiritual refuge.

Historical churches reveal a great deal about both their members and their community. My friend Jay has a special affinity for them and over the years, on our travels together, I've been to countless historical churches. The summer I lived in Williamsburg we'd go on long bicycle rides on Saturdays. These adventures often included a visit to a Colonial brick church. The Church of England, official church of the Virginia colony, maintained many small parish churches that still dot the countryside. One I particularly liked, Ware Church, sits in Gloucester, Virginia. Founded in 1680, the present building was erected between 1690 and 1713. Its simple yet elegant rectangular shape demonstrates the craftsmanship of both local and English artisans. The bricks, placed in a Flemish-bond pattern, show the wear of centuries. Its classic Georgian symmetry includes pediment doors and Palladian windows. A moss-covered brick wall surrounds the building and the churchyard includes graves with markers that date to the early eighteenth century.

Many cities in America boast a wealth of historic churches and synagogues in various states of decline. Certainly the old Eastern cities such as Boston, New York, Philadelphia, and Charleston feature an amazing number of these structures. As the populations of America's inner cities ebb and flow, the state of the old church buildings also changes. One haunting church sits in splendid isolation surrounded by blighted neighborhoods in northern Philadelphia. On one bike ride with Jay we took a detour to see a project his church had embarked upon. We jumped a low fence and walked into another place and time. St. James-the-Less parish church stands amid a sea of stone crosses, a copy of an English country church built in the thirteenth century. Construction began in 1846 and the vestry hoped the church would serve as an oasis for both the wealthy and the working classes. This vision to build a medieval-style church in the nineteenth century began a movement to build English Gothic churches across the American landscape. Today, its thick stone walls and vertical bell tower stand in slight decay, waiting for a new moment of glory. The carved wooden pews and elaborate high altar speak of exquisite craftsmanship, and its pastoral setting continues to be an oasis from the rough streets. A school has reopened on the surrounding property, and hopefully new activity will bring the church's restoration.

Sometimes adaptive reuse saves a historic church building. The Missouri Historical Society's library and research center, where I worked, is housed in the former United Hebrew Congregation synagogue. When the congregation moved west toward the suburbs, the Historical Society decided to buy the building. A beautiful domed room, once the sanctuary of the synagogue, now provides the library's patrons with a majestic place to read and research. A plaque on the wall indicates that Dr. Martin Luther King Jr. spoke at a meeting there during the 1960s.

While churches reveal rich history on the local level, the National Cathedral in Washington was built to tell America's story. With its flying buttresses and whimsical gargoyles the Gothic church sits on Mount Saint Alban, one of the highest spots in the city. Major Pierre L'Enfant, the city's original designer, envisioned a "great church for national purposes." Deemed the longest running construction project in Washington, work began on the building in 1907, when President Theodore Roosevelt laid the foundation stone. With the completion of the west towers in 1990 the building was considered finished. More than two hundred stained glass windows portray events in American and Christian history, including the Lewis and Clark expedition and the Iwo Jima flag raising. The popular space window honors the moon landing and includes a piece of lunar rock.

But the majority of America's churches are not architectural masterpieces. They are simple, small buildings that speak to their community's faith. Visitors with an inquisitive mind and a discerning eye will often discover a great deal of information about the past, such as how much value the congregation placed on architecture, opulence versus simplicity. Sometimes a church changes over time with its congregation. My church in St. Louis dated from the 1800s. The Presbyterians built it, then moved west. A Jewish congregation converted it to a synagogue. When that congregation moved, black Baptists bought it. Today it has come full circle and is Presbyterian again.

Reinterpreting a Hero's Grave

The second place of solitude I sought as I attempted to make a decision that day was William Clark's final resting place in Bellefontaine Cemetery, a large hilly graveyard north of downtown. The thirty-five-foot-tall gray granite obelisk sits atop a bluff overlooking an industrial park landscape of low buildings and train tracks loaded with freight cars. In the distance the Mississippi River flows toward downtown St. Louis and the Arch. I had visited Clark's grave on various occasions with different groups of people: good friends, work colleagues, teachers, and out-of-town guests. I was even privileged to visit it with one of Clark's biographers on his first visit to the grave.

When Clark died in 1838 he was buried on the outskirts of St. Louis at his nephew's farm. A grand funeral procession over a mile long carried his body to its burial place. When Bellefontaine cemetery opened in 1849, his family had his body moved there. His youngest son, Jefferson, died in 1900, and left money for the construction of a monument for his father's grave. The monument was officially dedicated four years later during the centennial of the Lewis and Clark expedition. It had always fascinated me because of the multiple messages it conveys, the foremost being a family's desire to honor a father and to pay tribute to his exalted place in our nation's history. The marker includes a large bust of Clark looking toward the confluence of the Mississippi and Missouri Rivers, the Lewis and Clark expedition's gateway to their exploration of western lands. Text underneath the bust reads: "William Clark, born in Virginia, August 1, 1770, entered into life eternal September 1, 1838. Soldier, Explorer, Statesman, and Patriot. His life is written in the history of his country." That final line always made me think. What does it mean exactly?

Most people don't think about grave markers as primary sources, but they can reveal many interesting things about both the person whose grave is marked and the people who created the marker. The historian Frederick Jackson Turner proclaimed the end of the American frontier in 1893, his so-called frontier thesis, published in a paper titled "The Significance of the Frontier in American History." Dedicated eleven years later, the Clark monument reveals much about sentiment in 1904 America. It boldly shouts Clark's role as trailblazer and flag bearer on the frontier. Carved on the monument are a bear head and a buffalo head, representing the large beasts the expedition encountered. A verse reads, "Behold, the Lord thy God hath set the land before thee: go up and possess it." It's taken from Deuteronomy 1:21, a biblical reference to God's command to the Israelites to conquer Canaan, the land he promised them. To early-twentieth-century Americans the message was no doubt very clear—the revival of the idea of Manifest Destiny signified acceptance of a seemingly God-ordained right of territorial expansion across the continent, coast to coast. Two additional quotations carved on the monument read, "The expedition of Lewis and Clark across the continent in 1804-5-6 [sic] marked the beginning of the process of exploration and colonization which thrust our national boundaries to the Pacific," and "This primary exploration through more than four thousand miles of savage wilderness planted the flag of the United States for the first time on the shores of the Pacific Ocean. It completed the extension of the United States across the vast western region of the American continent and gave us our outlook toward the Orient."

Over time, however, messages can change. One hundred years later, at the beginning of the bicentennial of the expedition in 2004, a group of Clark's descendants paid to refurbish the monument. They added another smaller stone several feet from the main marker that states that the original monument was a provision in Jefferson Kearny Clark's will and adds that the new stone "stands as a testimonial to the admiration and gratitude of William Clark's descendants and their fellow countrymen for his devotion to family and a lifetime of service to his country." One side features a quote by Clark from a letter written to Thomas Jefferson, dated December 15, 1825: "It is to be lamented that the deplorable situation of the Indians do [sic] not receive more of the human feelings of the nation." Sensitive to the cultural currents of a new age, Clark's descendants were no doubt embarrassed by the bold, aggressive language on the original monument. As the bicentennial events strived to cast the expedition in the new light of cultural exploration, even Clark's descendants felt it a good idea to reinterpret the original monument.

A Mysterious End

But what about Lewis's memory? Having seen Clark's grave, I had always wanted to visit Lewis's. Years later, I traveled to Nashville to present a workshop, and I seized the opportunity. On a rainy, damp late winter day, I drove south on the Natchez Trace Parkway, which follows the historic frontier road from Nashville to Natchez, Mississippi. The grayness seemed appropriate as Lewis's grave is adjacent to the spot where he died, surrounded by a fog of mystery and controversy. As I drove past wild turkeys and waterfalls, tobacco barns and misty vistas, the bucolic setting did not hint at the dangers of the trail in the early 1800s. All types of persons could be found traveling on the rough path, staying at the small inns (called stands) spaced about a day's walking distance from the next. At Grinder's stand, Lewis's life ended.

To this day there is no conclusive evidence as to whether his death was by his own hand or someone else's. Various historians have argued one theory or another over the decades, and in recent years Lewis descendants and others have petitioned the Park Service, stewards of the parkway and gravesite, to exhume the body and allow a forensic scientist to study the evidence in hopes of definitive proof of the cause of death. Park Service officials have denied the requests, citing the danger of disturbing nearby unmarked graves, among other reasons. Carolyn Gilman, curator of the Lewis and Clark exhibition, had concluded it was suicide, as did other prominent historians. Yet a review of the evidence reveals that a compelling case can be made for murder.

Those who had been closest to him, including Clark and President Jefferson, seemed to accept that he could have taken his life. Upon hearing the first reports of Lewis's death, Clark wrote, "I fear this report has too much truth . . . I fear, O! I fear the weight of his mind has overcome him. What will be the consequences?" Lewis's sudden death at the age of thirty-five shocked the nation that had only three years earlier celebrated the returning hero. Sadly, he had not managed to publish his journals from the expedition and thus leave his personal stamp on the final publication.

He is buried by the historic trace, and it is curious to me that his family did not move his body home to Virginia. The current grave marker did not appear until almost forty years after his death. In 1848 the state of Tennessee erected a twenty-foot-high stone monument, eight layers of rough stones topped by a broken shaft indicating a life cut short. It stands in stark contrast to Clark's grave. Surrounded by a swath of grass and trees, it is isolated. Unlike Clark's monument, it lacks sculptural flourishes and grandiose biblical passages. It simply states the dates of Lewis's life and his various roles, including commander of the expedition to the Oregon in 1803–1806.

Two statements etched on the memorial hint at the greatness of the grave's inhabitant: "In the language of Mr. Jefferson: his courage was undaunted; his firmness and perseverance yielded to nothing but impossibilities, a rigid disciplinarian yet tender as a father to those committed to his charge; honest, disinterested liberal with a sound understanding and a scrupulous fidelity to truth." The second inscription is in Latin: "Immaturus obi; sed tu felicior annos vive meos: Bona Republica! vive tuos" ("I died before my time, but thou O great and good Republic, live out my years while you live out your own").

History from a Cemetery

Over the years I've taught many workshops for teachers about using primary sources in the classroom and usually highlighted the four main types of sources used most by historians: documents, objects, photographs, and oral histories. One summer in St. Louis I taught a week-long teacher seminar focused on the Lewis and Clark story. We spent a day on each of the four sources, but on the fifth day I decided to try something different: a trip to Bellefontaine Cemetery. We discussed the words and images carved on Clark's monument, and the messages they conveyed about both Clark and the time period in which it was created. We were historians drawing conclusions about its designer, its builder, its materials, the person it honors, and the time period in which it was made.

Just as churches reveal a wealth of community history, a cemetery discloses much information about its community: who lived there, when it was settled, its religions, its occupations, and its wealth. Who is buried next to whom? Where is the cemetery located in relation to the community? What types of symbols are on the gravestones? Bellefontaine includes graves of the famous, such as the Busch mausoleums, architectural gems that hold the Busches of Anheuser-Busch fame; and the not so famous, such as Captain Isaiah Sellers, a steamboat captain on the Mississippi River for forty years, who supposedly used the pen name Mark Twain, inspiring author Samuel Clemens to do the same.

I've strolled through some truly fascinating cemeteries on my travels. Three of my favorites in the United States are Hollywood Cemetery in Richmond, Virginia; Copp's Hill Burying Ground in Boston, and Sleepy Hollow Cemetery in Concord, Massachusetts. Some cemeteries have become tourist destinations, like the Arlington National Cemetery across the Potomac from Washington DC and the cemeteries in New Orleans and Paris. One of the most compelling cemeteries I visited was in Zermatt, Switzerland. There, next to the town's main church spire, is a monument to those who died attempting to climb local mountains, including the Matterhorn. A small cemetery nearby includes the graves of those mountaineers, with stones carved with the symbols of mountaineering. The oldest dates to 1865, when four people died returning from the first successful expedition to reach the summit of the famous mountain.

In some ways, a walk through a cemetery is not that different than a walk through the National Portrait Gallery. Both feature snapshots of biography and offer an interpretation of the person, through a statement or carved symbols. Sometimes the gravestone is designed by others, other times by the subject himself. The elaborate stones of colonial graves in the Concord cemetery are filled with winged skulls, winged heads, and sunbursts, along with Bible verses or brief descriptions of the person. The symbols appear over and over again, but it is the words that eloquently personalize the gravestones. The colonial stones hint at an acceptance of death that shocks modern sensibilities. Sometimes the stone's design fails to fit the image one has of the person. It may be overdesigned or stunning in its simplicity. Calvin Coolidge's simple grave reveals his sentiments in life. He had risen to the most powerful position in the country, but in the end preferred a simple stone with his name and life dates and the presidential seal. To the history educator, a cemetery offers any number of teaching opportunities and a rare window to the past.

Decision Point

Standing in front of Clark's grave with its carved buffalo and grizzly heads, I made my decision. I would accept the job offer and move back east. I had unexpectedly enjoyed my time in St. Louis and had learned to truly appreciate the places and traditions that define the city. I became a Cardinals fan, ate Ted Drewes frozen custard, witnessed the restoration of glorious Forest Park, and gawked at the large mansions of the Central West End. I'd visited the Anheuser-Busch brewery and threw snowballs to the polar bears at the zoo during a wintery encounter. I'd even tried my hand at movie acting, landing a small part in a locally filmed movie and attending the premiere at the Tivoli Theatre. But I'd never understood the constant obsession with the 1904 St. Louis World's Fair and the overused designation "first . . . west of the Mississippi" sprinkled proudly throughout the region. I couldn't satisfactorily answer the common question asked at St. Louis parties, "Where did you go to high school?" and really couldn't understand why a conversation would usually die when I said I'd moved from Washington. Was

Washington really such an alien place? I'd tired of a landscape that seemed monotonous to my East Coast eyes and had grown weary of the city's distance from other major urban hubs. I would greatly miss the dear friends I made there, but I was ready to leave Lewis and Clark and move on to new adventures in history.

15
WE'RE FLYING OVER HELL STRETCH?

> The purpose of this letter is to impress upon you as
> an Air Mail pilot that the Department places a very
> high value indeed upon your life and upon the lives
> of your brother pilots, and that the Department
> is particularly anxious that every possible
> safety measure be injected into this service.
>
> —*Paul Henderson, Second*
> *Assistant Postmaster General*

Everyone's road through life has unexpected curves. Like most people, I didn't plot a specific career course, and as a result my journey has taken at least two rather surprising turns. One was St. Louis. I never expected to live in the Midwest and work on a Lewis and Clark exhibition. The other was a job at the National Air and Space Museum in Washington. While it is one of the world's most visited museums, it was not one of my favorites in Washington. I thought the subject matter narrow and limiting and was sometimes bothered by the celebratory nature of the exhibitions, which often failed to engage me because of their focus on technology over people.

When the Lewis and Clark job ended, the East Coast beckoned again and I decided it would be easier to return to somewhere I'd already lived than to forge into new territory. Plus I like Washington and as I've said earlier, there is no more stimulating environment than the Smithsonian. As I've also said, it's hard to get hired, even with connections. Could I find a way back? I felt that I had earned the right to be somewhat choosy in selecting my next job—I wanted promotion potential, supervisory responsibility, and exhibition development work. A position that matched my skills and criteria became available at the Air and Space Museum, so I decided to apply. After a long period of waiting and what seemed like divine intervention, I was offered the job. I made my decision that day in the St. Louis cemetery and accepted a position at a museum that had previously held little allure for me.

So, one day several years after standing on the Lewis and Clark trail in the Bitterroot Mountains of Montana, I found myself at lunch with descendants of the Wright Brothers, discussing the importance of preserving the memory of Katherine, Orville and Wilbur's sister. Not long after, in front of a large audience, I interviewed a shuttle astronaut, asking him what it was like to sit on the launch pad. My history journey had once again taken a radical turn.

Icons of Flight

The Smithsonian's National Air and Space Museum sits at the foot of Capitol Hill in a prime location on the National Mall. President Gerald Ford officially opened the building on July 1, 1976, a bicentennial gift to the nation. The museum is a temple to America's achievements in air and space technology—those machines that have gone faster, higher, and farther. Attendance has far exceeded expectations over the years and currently stands at eight million visitors annually.

The museum holds an amazing draw on the tourist psyche. During the high tourist season, lines of excited visitors line up to enter its cavernous halls and see missiles, satellites, and aircraft of all shapes and sizes. As they pass through the main doors, they gaze in wonder at the icons of aerospace: Chuck Yeager's orange Bell X-1 *Glamorous Glennis*, the *Spirit of St. Louis*, the Apollo 11 command module, and an X-15. Museum curator Tom Crouch has written that "aviation and space flight have the capacity to capture our imaginations, symbolizing as they do the power of technology to realize ancient dreams, overcome obstacles once regarded as insuperable, and provide an unparalleled sense of power and control."

The never-ending sea of humanity coming through the doors is a source of wonderment to me. What draws so many people to this place? Do that many people really like airplanes? Or, is it *the* place to go? Its coolness factor cannot be denied. The National Museum of American History's treasures just can't compete with gleaming machines that broke speed records or traveled beyond the earth. Is it because these objects speak a unique American story so attractive to many foreign visitors? No museum anywhere in the world can display such an incredible collection of space-related artifacts. Whatever the reasons, there remains a mystery to flight that continues to inspire wonder. As historian Joseph Corn wrote, "For not a few visitors, however, the Museum still functions as a shrine to flight, a place to pay homage to the machines that have miraculously broken free of earth's bondage and entered the heavens."

An Obscure Historical Marker

One early spring evening after work, I exited the museum onto Independence Avenue and turned right into the setting sun. As I walked west toward the Jefferson Memorial, more and more people crowded the sidewalk, all going in the same direction. The swarm was headed toward the cherry trees at peak bloom, an annual rite of spring for many Washington residents who can withstand the tens of thousands of tourists that throng West Potomac Park. Anyone who has ever witnessed the massive puffs of pink in the warm air never forgets the sight. Cherry blossoms, Independence Day fireworks, and perhaps an Inauguration are the three Washington events that everyone should experience at least once in their life, if they can deal with crowds.

The cherry trees ring the Tidal Basin and I planned to walk the loop around the basin, something I'd done many times, but this year my goal was different. I'd just heard about an obscure stone marker sitting along the Potomac River several hundred yards from the basin and near the FDR Memorial. I couldn't believe I had never heard about the marker.

"I'm such a history geek," I muttered to myself. "Tens of thousands of people are headed in this direction to exalt in the beauty of nature, and I'm excited to see a historic marker."

I veered away from the pink trees, heading toward the river, and soon found the stone marker and its metal plaque. Erected in 1958 by the Aero Club of Washington to mark an auspicious fortieth anniversary, it read: "The world's first airplane mail to be operated as a continuously scheduled public service started from this field May 15, 1918." President Wilson and other dignitaries had stood in West Potomac Park providing the official send-off for a lone army pilot in his Curtiss "Jenny" biplane. This was the inauguration of the Post Office's regular service between Washington and New York, a three-hour flight. Unfortunately, the pilot, Lt. George Boyle, had a little problem along the way. He got lost. Using a road map and a faulty compass to navigate, he ended up in Waldorf, Maryland, south of Washington. The plane flipped upon landing and was damaged, so Boyle couldn't reach his intended destination. However, the flight from New York arrived safely, and the Post Office's Air Mail Service had begun.

Most people have no idea that the story of commercial aviation begins with airmail. I did not know this when I started several years of work developing a new exhibition about the history of air transportation in the United States. While the first airline started service in 1914 (only eleven years after the Wright Brothers' initial flight!) it quickly folded because it could not fly enough passengers or cargo to stay in business. Other airlines tried and failed, including those that flew people to Cuba during Prohibition. The U.S. government, though, recognized the potential of air travel and began to experiment with airmail service. The Post Office first approved an experimental flight to carry mail in 1911 to demonstrate the potential of using airplanes to transport mail. Seven years later the U.S. Air Mail Service began. The airmail pilots were young and bold. Of the more than two hundred pilots the Post Office hired in the first eight years, thirty-six died flying the mail. We wanted to tell the story of these airmail pilots.

In the beginning the pilots flew mostly JN-4s, commonly called Jennys, training planes from World War I. The engines were unreliable, navigation instruments were basic, and landing gear could not support rough landings. The pilots flew close to the ground to navigate from landmark to landmark—a process called contact flying. Of course when clouds were low, vision was difficult, and mountainous terrain especially exacerbated the challenge.

My Map Quest

One day while researching the "America by Air" exhibition I stumbled upon an image of a map on the National Postal Museum's Web site. The hand-drawn map by an early airmail pilot named James Murray is in the collection of the National Archives. The map depicts a section of the early transcontinental airmail route laid out in 1920. Most researchers will admit that from time to time they become fixated on a certain document or object that catches their fancy. Keeping true to character, I became fascinated with this map—I had to see it. Any historian will tell you that a research trail often leads to unexpected places. My quest for this map led me on an exciting journey.

The National Archives building sits on Constitution Avenue, an easy walk across the National Mall from the Air and Space Museum.

I knew that the map lay somewhere in its depths. Unfortunately the researcher at the Postal Museum who had found it did not document its location very well. This meant my investigative skills would be put to the test. The Postal Museum historian tried to help narrow my search, but ultimately I spent days looking through file after file of schedules, personnel records, and forced landing reports. Dull as this may sound, the forced landing reports especially yielded vital information about the challenges faced by those early pilots. They were standard government forms with blank lines filled in with the pilot's handwritten reason of why he landed the plane in an unscheduled location. The excuses were fascinating and ran the gamut from rain, snow, and hail to engine failure, instrument failure, pilot failure (getting lost!), and my favorite—"hit a duck on take-off and was forced to land. I dug it out of the radiator, straightened the bent slat and continued on."

On day three of my search, I opened a file and there was the map—in the personnel files, the very location it wasn't supposed to be. What sweet victory. I tried to imagine the map in the hands of young James Murray as he flew over Pennsylvania. How long did it take him to draw the map? I learned later that he had made the map to enter in a contest sponsored by the Postal Service. And he had won.

Flying over Hell Stretch

As the team began to think about the concepts we wanted to convey in the exhibition, we decided that it was important to show the challenges of early navigation and to discuss the concept of contact flying. On his map Murray had carefully drawn the various landmarks a pilot would spot as he flew the route. As with the Star-Spangled Banner activity, I decided to try to find a way to make the map the focus of an activity. I wanted museum visitors to have the opportunity to examine the map. Why not challenge them to put the landmarks in the correct order, as if flying along the route? To accomplish this, I'd need aerial photos of several landmarks.

Locating historical photos would prove much more difficult than I had imagined.

I spent the following year tracking down photos, looking in a variety of archives and libraries. The more archives I called, the more I began to realize that such photos may not exist. The activity I had developed would not work without photos, so I needed a plan B. Our budget did not allow us to hire a helicopter, but along came a friend of the museum who owned a helicopter and offered to take me and a Smithsonian photographer to Pennsylvania for a photo shoot. I contacted the State College, Pennsylvania, chapter of the EAA (Experimental Aircraft Association) and was put in touch with an excellent source, a man named Bob Hines. Bob offered to be our guide—he had flown over the territory for many years and knew it well. He assured me that most of the landmarks still existed.

So, on a clear crisp day in mid-April I hopped into a twin-engine helicopter on the grassy bank of a cove of the Potomac River south of Washington. This was my first helicopter trip and my pilots, a father and son, assured me it would be a smooth ride. We buckled up, started the engines, and rose up into the cloudless Virginia sky. The pilots carefully navigated through the busy airways of Northern Virginia, around Dulles Airport and over the Potomac into Maryland airspace. Our first stop was Montgomery County Airport, where we picked up our photographer, my colleague Eric. Then we headed toward Pennsylvania.

In studying our route I had realized that we would fly in the vicinity of Gettysburg, and the pilots graciously accommodated my request to fly over the battlefield, a place I had visited many times in my youth. The Pennsylvania memorial rose grandly from the brilliant green field. Here and there a white or pink dogwood stood out in stark contrast from the green. While we zoomed over the grounds, I tried to recognize the various areas of the battlefield—the peach orchard, Little Round Top, Devil's Den, the unfinished railroad bed, and Seminary Ridge. I wanted to say, "Wait! Let's do a loop or two over the fields." But we were on a mission of a different era.

Gradually the land transformed from rolling hills to sharp wooded ridges as we came to the Allegheny Mountains. We had reached "Hell Stretch," the infamous section of the transcontinental airmail route that claimed the lives of many airmail pilots. More fatal accidents occurred along this stretch of the transcontinental route than any other. The first Superintendent of the Air Mail Service, Benjamin Lipsner, described Hell Stretch as follows: "The route across the Allegheny Mountains was considered by some the ultimate in dangerous flying, and by others it was called absolutely impossible. Later this stretch became known as the 'graveyard' or 'hell stretch,' and famous pilots then and even later declared that transporting passengers across it would never be safe or practical." The mountains look tame compared to the Rocky Mountains, but the changing weather patterns surrounding them resulted in challenging wind currents and foggy conditions. Pilots were often forced to fly low to see the ground, a practice that is especially dangerous in mountainous terrain. The lack of emergency landing fields meant a forced landing was nearly impossible on the wooded hillsides.

We landed at the State College airport on the edge of Penn State University, in Nittany Lion territory. After fueling the helicopter and greeting Bob, we were ready. Eric wanted to take the doors off to ensure better photographs, so we all agreed that we could handle a chilly ride.

We first headed northeast to Bellefonte. From 1919 to 1927 the town's airfield was the first refueling stop on the historic transcontinental airmail route stretching from Long Island, New York, to San Francisco. The flight from New York to Bellefonte covered 215 miles. Today the former landing field is the site of a Penn DOT garage and the Bellefonte Area High School. The picturesque town square features an elaborate white-columned courthouse with a classic cupola topped by a weathervane. Local legend says pilot Slim Lewis once buzzed the courthouse so close that the weathervane spun around.

We next headed east toward Sunbury, looking for a white fire tower drawn on Murray's map. Bob thought it still stood as the directions said, "on the crest of the last mountain to the north on leaving the pass"—Woodward Pass, but it looked like telecommunications antennas had taken its place. Strike one. We continued on and the mountains leveled out to rolling hills and a seemingly unchanged pastoral landscape of small towns. From our altitude of several thousand feet, the scenery spread below lacked clear evidence of the twenty-first century . . . it could have been 1921.

At Sunbury we veered right, flying down the Susquehanna River to a small airport for a fueling stop. We took photos of two landmarks on the map: islands in the river and railroad tracks at the river's edge. As we flew I looked down at the changing landforms. The main topographical feature in that area is the mighty Susquehanna River. How peaceful it looked from above. I thought of what Anne Morrow Lindbergh wrote about rivers in her book *North to the Orient*:

> Rivers perhaps are the only physical features of the world that are at their best from the air. Mountain ranges, no longer seen in profile, dwarf to anthills; seas lose their horizons; lakes have no longer depth but look like bright pennies on the earth's surface; forests become a thin impermanent film, a moss on the top of a wet stone, easily rubbed off. But rivers, which from the ground one usually sees only in cross sections, like a small sample of ribbon—rivers stretch out serenely ahead as far as the eye can reach. Rivers are seen in their true stature. . . . [A]nd they remain, permanent, possessive. Next to them, man's gleaming cement roads which he has built with such care look fragile as paper streamers thrown over the hills, easily blown away. Even the railroads seem only scratched in with a penknife. But rivers have carved their way over the earth's face for centuries and they will stay.

Up until this point we hadn't been following the exact route of the map, but upon returning to Sunbury, we changed course, turning due west to follow the designated route and continue our search for the landmarks Murray had drawn. As the navigator I called out each landmark and all eyes scanned the area for it.

"A racetrack should be somewhere to the south."

"There it is"—someone's excellent eyes had spotted an overgrown oval track, which hadn't been used in decades. *Click* went Eric's camera.

Despite the fact that we were in a helicopter, blades whirring above us, we felt a powerful connection to early airmail pilots as we replicated their journey, seeing their landscape. We were in our own time machine, the sound of wind in our ears. The decision to take the doors off yielded two results. The first was Eric's crystal-clear photographs. The second was our chattering teeth. Eric later admitted that he thought he would never thaw out. How foolish of us not to wear our leather flight suits! I exhorted my fellow travelers that, thanks to our open air flight, we had come even closer to feeling what those pilots experienced in their open cockpits.

"Red covered bridge to the south." *Click.*

As we headed back to the State College airport, we had one last landmark to photograph. "A lone mountain may be seen to the south just across the Pennsylvania Railroad tracks." On the map it was marked Egg Hill, and it was easy to spot—sticking up out of the rolling hills without other mountains in the vicinity.

Before we left State College, we drove to Bellefonte and the American Philatelic Society, the national headquarters for the largest non-profit society of stamp collectors in the world. Bob Hines's uncle had collected a magnificent variety of photographs of local airmail activity from the glory days of Bellefonte, and many of them were on display in an exhibit. On the grounds of the society headquarters, near the bank of a creek, stands a nine-foot-tall granite monument dedicated to the early U.S. airmail pilots and specifically to the thirty-four pilots who lost their lives on Hell Stretch.

Meet Wild Bill

One of those pilots became iconic to the exhibition team because of a classic photograph taken of him standing in his leather flight suit, feet apart, left hand behind his back, right hand holding a cigarette, helmet on, goggles pulled above the light-colored eyes that stared into the camera—the James Dean of pilots. "Wild Bill" Hopson was a larger-than-life pilot who was almost thirty-three years old when he joined the Air Mail Service in 1920. He "epitomized everything that was glamorous and reckless about the early pilots." Author Bonny Farmer writes that on one occasion, in order to keep a date, Hopson hitched a ride on a loaded plane flying from Bellefonte to New York. He sat on the wing of the plane, holding tightly to the guy wires. Supposedly he dropped love letters weighted with bolts to a young woman on the way, the girlfriend of an air field clerk— as a favor.

During his flying career Hopson set two speed records and made the first night flight from Omaha to Chicago. He also made more than the average number of forced landings, including one where he got caught in an electrical and wind storm, the motor cut out, and his plane tore down a hundred-yard swath of an Iowa farmer's cornfield. He didn't earn the nickname "Wild Bill" for nothing. In July 1920 Postal Superintendent Colyer wrote, "I have received several reports from various fields of continuous spectacular flying on your part. . . . I have numerous reports of your stunting mail ships. This is absolutely against regulations and further actions of this kind will merit disciplinary action." While there was talk among his superiors of firing him, Wild Bill managed to survive until the postal service stopped flying the mail in 1927.

The business of flying the mail was turned over to contract companies. Many of the pilots went to work for them, including Hopson, who was assigned to the New York–Chicago route, which included Hell Stretch, and that is where his career came to an abrupt end. In October 1928, while flying low in heavy rain, Hopson apparently struck a dead chestnut tree sticking up out of a wooded hill and crashed near Polk, Pennsylvania. He had been carrying a heavy load of mail and only ten pounds were salvageable. Major newspapers across the country first reported him missing, then announced his death. Then they uncovered a new story: "Ill-Fated Plane Yields

$65,000 in Diamonds," "Diamonds in Burned Mail Plane Bring Rush." The Associated Press reported that Hopson had been carrying jewels worth $100,000 and that diamonds worth $65,000 had been picked from the wreckage by eager locals. The *New York Times* called it a diamond rush and reported that "women tore their silk stockings and bespattered dresses with mud in the scramble for the gems." One woman found fourteen diamonds. Eventually a postal inspector arrived to track down the diamonds, but rumors persisted that not all had been found.

Hopson lost his life on that hillside doing what he loved. He had flown the mail for eight years and had traveled over four hundred thousand miles, second only to one other pilot. Several days later humorist Will Rogers supposedly paid tribute to Hopson in a St. Louis newspaper. He credited Hopson with saving his life during an earlier flight. "So 'Hoppie,' Old Boy, here's hoping you are piloting the best cloud the Boss has got in his hangar up there, and you don't have to worry about low ceiling, engine missing, head winds, or even whether the old rip cord will pull in case.—Yours, Will Rogers." In a sad note of irony, Rogers himself would die in an airplane crash less than ten years later.

Los Angeles Times columnist Harry Carr also wrote a moving tribute to Hopson and all airmail pilots. "These young adventurers who fly the mails are the real heroes of our day. It is one thing to do stunt flying with a grand stand full of people yelling their heads off; but it is another thing to take these lonely perils of the darkness and the night as a matter of tiresome routine. We drop a stamped envelope into the mail box with a five cent stamp; and these pilots dedicate their young lives to the ordeal of seeing that it gets there."

Today Wild Bill's life-size photo stands prominently in the "America by Air" exhibition at the National Air and Space Museum, the subject of hundreds of photographs taken by visitors who pose with this cooler-than-cool early pilot. Visitors can learn about contact flying by examining James Murray's map and the aerial photographs we took. And brave visitors can even make flight decisions like early airmail pilots in a "Fly the Mail" computer interactive based on the records in the National Archives. They experience the various kinds of obstacles faced by those intrepid pilots and, along the way, may even hit a duck.

I, too, achieved some kind of Smithsonian immortality in that my face, hands, and ears were cast for a model of an airmail pilot that sits near Wild Bill. On the figure's knee is a scrolling kneeboard with a map. Perhaps he is trying to figure his course through Hell Stretch.

16
HOW LUCKY WAS LINDY?

I was conscious again of the fundamental magic of
flying . . . for not only is life put in new patterns from
the air, but it is somehow arrested, frozen into form.

—*Anne Morrow Lindbergh*

When I moved to St. Louis, I quickly became aware that several
events in the past continue to hold deep roots in the sentimental
consciousness of the residents. The Lewis and Clark expedition,
the focus of my stay in Missouri, is one. Another is the 1904 World's
Fair held one hundred years after Lewis and Clark passed through
the city. In many ways the fair signified the pinnacle of St. Louis's
potential, when the city stood on the verge of true greatness and
for one brief moment held the nation's attention. The third event
is really a person . . . Charles Lindbergh.

In 1925 young Lindbergh moved to St. Louis as an airmail pilot
and began a relationship with the city that lasted a lifetime. He

managed to convince several businessmen to invest in his dream to fly solo across the Atlantic. On May 21, 1927, he landed in Paris and won the $25,000 Orteig Prize for this feat. He also became an instant worldwide celebrity, the subject of newspaper headlines around the globe. St. Louis residents joyously shared in this moment of personal triumph: Lindbergh's plane, the *Spirit of St. Louis*, was named for their city. Upon his return, Lindbergh was welcomed with a seven-mile parade, five hundred thousand people lining the route. Lindbergh allowed the Missouri Historical Society to display his extensive collection of trophies, awards, and gifts, which more than a hundred thousand people viewed in the first four days. (Lindbergh eventually donated the collection to the society.)

During my time in St. Louis, however, I knew little about Lindbergh. I drove down Lindbergh Boulevard often, walked under the replica of the *Spirit of St. Louis* hanging in the Missouri History Museum atrium, and viewed a special Lindbergh exhibition there. But, despite the fact that my condo stood several blocks away from where Lindbergh had met with his investors, and my desk overlooked the hill in Forest Park where thousands had gathered to watch him perform aerial maneuvers, my historical interests were firmly focused on another century. Ironically, though, my next place of employment also owned a collection of Lindbergh items and featured a *Spirit of St. Louis* (the real one) hanging in its entrance. Three years into my job at the National Air and Space Museum, my focus suddenly shifted to Lindbergh as I began work on a new exhibition called "Pioneers of Flight."

Packing with Lindbergh

You can tell something about a person by observing the way he packs. Is he efficient, a spatial thinker? Does she throw it all in at the last minute? Does she make lists? Obviously not all journeys require the same preparation. I love to travel but hate to pack. Fortunately, unlike Charles Lindbergh, I will never have to pack for a flight thousands of miles over wilderness.

In the spring of 1931 Lindbergh began packing for a trip that would take him and his wife, Anne, from Canada, across Alaska, and over the Pacific Ocean to Asia. Meticulous to a fault, he tried to anticipate every possible emergency scenario, from a forced landing in the middle of the ocean to a crash in the northern wilderness. They would be visiting Eskimo villages where Anne was the first Caucasian woman the villagers had ever seen and also attending embassy parties in the capitals of Asia. Anne observed that Lindbergh turned packing into a science of prioritizing. As she put it, "Every object to be taken had to be weighed, mentally as well as physically. The weight in pounds must balance the value in usefulness." She wrote that her husband "added and subtracted endlessly from lists."

They sorted things into three piles: necessities, discards, and a pile representing items that needed to be put in one of the other two piles. They allowed themselves only eighteen pounds each for personal items. Anne admitted that shoes were the most weight-expensive item in personal baggage. She took only two pairs. She later wrote that her husband "always packed up the equipment himself and took great pride in the neat orderly way in which it all fitted down and presented an even surface which could be covered by the canvas flaps and strapped in place. I was never allowed to touch it in case I should put the bag of emergency medicines or delicate instruments down underneath the cans of tomatoes or the tool kit."

The purpose of the flight was to survey the great circle route, from New York to Tokyo, as a possible flight path for commercial airlines. Lindbergh was organizing and financing the trip, but would report to Pan American Airways when he returned. Another flight two years later covered four continents and served the same purpose.

The challenge for us as exhibition developers was to figure out how to best tell the story of these flights. "Pioneers of Flight" featured the colorful personalities of the years between the two world wars, when "airmindedness," the mind-set that flying was here to stay and held great potential to transform society, blossomed. The exhibition included some of the most amazing aircraft in the museum's collection, packed in a layered effect into a small gallery. At the center of the exhibition sat Amelia Earhart's bright red Lockheed Vega, what she called her "little red bus," star of her famous solo transatlantic flight in 1932.

Overhead, its massive wings spreading across the gallery, loomed the Fokker T-2, first to fly nonstop across the United States in 1923. Thirty feet away hung Lindbergh's *Spirit of St. Louis*, one of the most famous objects in the museum's collection. The Douglas World Cruiser *Chicago*, the first plane to circle around the world, sat next to the seaplane Curtiss R3C-2, in which Jimmy Doolittle was presented the prestigious Schneider Trophy for winning a speed race meant to encourage technical advances in aviation. Each aircraft had been front page news in its day and had fascinating stories to tell.

Nearby sat the Lindberghs' Lockheed Sirius. I had walked by this dust-covered black plane with red wings hundreds of times. Its pontoons rested on a wooden platform, keeping it safely out of the reach of visitors' hands. Surrounded by such great company, the two-seat plane seemed to get lost in the iconic crowd. Painted carefully in two-inch capital letters on each side in front of the cockpit was "TINGMISSARTOQ," the Eskimo word for "one who flies like a bird." An Eskimo boy had painted the name on the plane during a layover in Greenland.

When the Lindberghs, Charles at the controls of the Lockheed Sirius, taxied away from the wharf in Flushing Bay, Long Island, on a hot July day in 1931, they would once again become the subject of newspaper headlines around the world for their entire trip. Their travels served as a vicarious way for readers to find adventure. Charles and Anne left one-year-old Charlie behind. "I would have been content to stay home and do nothing else but care for my baby, but there were those survey flights that lured us to more adventures. I went on them proudly, taking my place as a crew member," wrote Anne. "The beauty and mystery of flying never palled." She later documented the trips in two wonderfully written bestselling books *North to the Orient* and *Listen, the Wind!*

Brought into the Light

When developing an exhibition, the curator usually takes the lead in deciding which artifacts will be included, though other members of the team offer suggestions. As the audience expert, my contribution is to help the team members think through the different stories they may want to tell and the various mediums to convey them, ensuring that a variety of visitors will learn something. The process often begins with the content experts developing a preliminary artifact list to discuss with the team. Sometimes the audience experts will argue for a specific artifact that tells a story that may resonate with a certain age group or will suggest a certain storyline be included. We want our visitors to see themselves in our exhibitions.

Since we were updating an existing "Pioneers" gallery, the initial artifact list included the main Lindbergh artifacts from the previous display. But the curator remembered a magnificent collection of over a hundred items in storage that Lindbergh had saved from his journeys in the plane. The equipment and unused supplies had never before been on public display in Washington. Was now the time to bring them out and put them on view? Was there space for them? What story would they help us tell?

The designer wanted to place the *Tingmissartoq* in a setting. It is normally displayed as a seaplane, with floats instead of wheels, so we decided to tie the plane to a wooden dock and use lighting to simulate water. The supplies and equipment would be spread out on the dock as if the Lindberghs were packing for the trip. The display could demonstrate the amount of detail with which Lindbergh planned his trips—and encourage visitors to explore the great variety of items needed for every emergency scenario. It would provide a glimpse into Lindbergh's mind. More perceptive visitors might also note the comparison between Lindbergh and Amelia Earhart, who was not known for her careful planning. There are good reasons why Lindbergh never found himself in a back-to-the-wall situation.

The dock would become not a static display of artifacts, but an active area of exploration where visitors could open doors to packing crates, discern the purpose of some of the objects, decipher Morse code, and use a computer activity to make packing decisions like the Lindberghs. Thrilled with the prospect for such engagement, the educators on the team eagerly offered to help the content expert. After a careful review of the collections database, team members scheduled a research trip to the collections storage area to view the items.

Behind Closed Doors

There's a mysterious aura surrounding the storage areas of the Smithsonian. Several popular movies have depicted vast vaults under the National Mall. Unfortunately or fortunately, depending on how you look at it, a scriptwriter's imagination does not match reality. People always jump at an opportunity to see "behind the scenes" at the Smithsonian. I'm never sure what they think they will see. They probably expect to find the Holy Grail. But behind most of the "staff only" doors are offices with people sitting at computers, meeting rooms with conference tables, and libraries filled with, well, shelves of books.

Of course it's not all boring office space. What people really hope to see is the cool stuff that is not on display. Since most of the museums have at least some amount of storage on site, there are unexpected surprises in the deep dark corners of the Smithsonian. In the Natural History Museum, just around the corner from the public areas, are corridors lined with cabinets full of bone specimens, dead birds, butterflies, strange things in jars, and all kinds of creepy objects. The creative storage of items is an art form, with things stored in every nook and cranny. The American History Museum includes storage rooms scattered throughout the building full of carefully catalogued items of every shape and size, from political campaign buttons to Muppets. Other museums are no different. I once visited the Academy of Natural Sciences in Philadelphia as part of my Lewis and Clark work. Like most natural history museums, its collection areas were a maze of cabinets. My guide pulled out a drawer filled with blue bird specimens, while another drawer held green birds. On several occasions I was allowed to see the state-of-the-art storage for the Lewis and Clark plant specimens. Kept in a climate-controlled room, each one was carefully packed in an acid-free folder. Despite the sterile environment, the power of the object shone through. It didn't take long for my mind to imagine Meriwether Lewis standing in the sunshine along the banks of the Clearwater River picking some ponderosa pine needles or some camas flowers in Weippe Prairie.

Not surprisingly, given the size of its objects, the National Air and Space Museum does not have much storage at its Mall building. For decades a collection of old hangar buildings called the Garber Facility, located in Maryland, housed an eclectic assortment of plane parts, models, and popular history items. The facility was named for Paul Garber, the man responsible in no small part for collecting more than half of the over 350 airplanes in the Smithsonian collection, including the *Spirit of St Louis*. He was quick to send a cable to Lindbergh in Paris congratulating him on his accomplishment and suggesting that he might want to donate the plane to the Smithsonian. The engine was probably still warm when the telegram arrived. Talk about foresight!

The Garber Facility used to be open to the public and the airplane enthusiasts I know talk fondly about tours of the place. Usually only the most hardcore of plane enthusiasts visited, so they didn't mind the four- or five-hour tours. The opening of the museum's Steven F. Udvar-Hazy Center in 2003, a huge hangar the size of several football fields in Chantilly, Virginia, allowed much more of the collection to be displayed and brought an end to public access at Garber. (A more recent addition to the center means that most of the collections storage will eventually be in Virginia.) While most people relish the grand variety of gleaming airplanes on display at the Udvar-Hazy Center, I know there are those who long for the days when people could walk through the workshop environment of Garber and talk to the plane restorers. Fortunately, now visitors can observe work in action through large windows providing views of the state-of-the-art restoration shop and display area at the Udvar-Hazy Center.

Bringing Hidden Treasures to Light

While my work does not take me to the Garber Facility very often, my visits there are always rewarding. With hundreds of shelves and drawers and all manner of storage containers, plus large items sitting wrapped under plastic awaiting restoration, Garber offers an allure and the promise of undiscovered treasure for those of us who do not work in the collections division.

That day at Garber, we donned white gloves to protect the items from our oily skin and one of the collections staff started opening drawers and unwrapping packages. As I stood there looking through the storage cabinets, a sense of déjà vu overcame me. Perusing the assorted emergency equipment and camping supplies, I realized that seven years earlier I had been researching the equipment that Lewis and Clark had packed for their famous expedition 126 years before the Lindberghs' flight—two totally different expeditions of exploration with different purposes and modes of transportation, but both traveling through foreign cultures and into remote territory. Both saw their share of snow and mosquitoes. While one would assume that the packing lists would be totally different, there were some similarities—sextant, octant, matches, dried food, and so on. Both expeditions were planned by men who were detail-oriented and meticulous, as well as flexible, and both expeditions proved successful.

My Favorite Artifacts

With every exhibition I work on, I become fascinated with specific artifacts. This time it was the armbrust cup. This strange cloth-covered oval object, worn over the face, converted condensation from breath into drinking water—for use in emergency landings at sea. Since weight restrictions were an ever-present challenge, the Lindberghs could take only a limited supply of water. Lindbergh had read about this new invention before his solo flight across the Atlantic and, not willing to wait until the product went into production, had paid inventor C. W. Armbrust $50 for one of his handmade prototypes to take on the journey. He also took several along on the trips in the *Tingmissartoq*. There is no record that he or Anne used them, thanks to smooth flights, but no doubt their presence helped provide some peace of mind. Obviously he considered them worth their added weight. The device looks uncomfortable to wear and belongs in the "hope I never have to use" category.

The correct name of the artifact proved a point of confusion for the team. We encountered several spellings. In her books, Anne listed it as an "armburst" cup. Finally we found an official answer. Our curator did some sleuthing and found the original patent given to Charles W. Armbrust in 1931. Mr. Armbrust had filed for a patent in 1926, the year before Lindbergh's solo flight, describing the goal of his invention: "to provide an efficient and simple water conserving device which can be carried on board of sea going vessels as a part of the life saving equipment, and whereby persons shipwrecked or afloat on the sea or in desert places without fresh water, can supply themselves with a limited quantity of pure condensed water from the exhaled breath."

Another artifact that intrigued me was the sled. I was surprised to learn that the Lindberghs had taken an eleven-foot-long, fifty-pound wooden sled along, carefully disassembled into sections and designed so that the parts could be tied together with leather thongs. In case of emergency landing on Greenland's ice cap, the Lindberghs would be prepared. The sled could carry a month's supply of food, a rifle, a pistol, ammunition, fishing gear, and other supplies. It took the staff several days to locate the large crate that held the sled. It was buried behind stacks of artifacts and had not been opened in many years, if ever. We carefully opened the crate and lifted the lid, finding the sled wrapped in plastic. Several pairs of snowshoes were sitting on top. It was a goose bump moment. The sled was in excellent condition and required only minimal conservation work.

Ultimately, just like the Lindberghs, we had to make some tough choices because we simply didn't have the space to display all of the items in this collection. We based our final decisions on several factors. Was the artifact in good condition? How much conservation work would it require? Some items, due to their materials, had unfortunately deteriorated over the years and were in poor condition. A second factor was the story we planned to tell. We wanted to display a variety of items and to convey the different emergency scenarios that Lindbergh had tried to anticipate. There was a sail and a mast from the rubber boat in case of emergency landing at sea, but no boat. There were wool-covered canteens, flying caps and goggles, mosquito netting, pith helmets, flashlights, matches, a tent, blankets, navigational equipment, heated flight suits, stocking boots, gloves, mittens, parkas, raincoats, ice crampons, thread, needles, insect repellant and spray guns, medical supplies, tools for the plane, a machete, an alpine ax, a kerosene lantern, a Primus (oil-burning) stove, radio equipment, and even a rubber inflatable globe (which, sadly, had deteriorated beyond repair). And then there was the food: corned beef, canned butter, canned tomatoes, baked beans, canned and powdered milk, canned pork and canned tongue, bouillon cubes, dried soup, and the granola bars of the day, Horlick's malted milk lunch tablets "for army and navy use, sportsmen, athletes, travelers, etc.," as the can advertised.

I perused the drawers of items and wondered how they had all fit. The storage compartments are not obvious. Even more puzzling was the fact that on various occasions the Lindberghs slept overnight on the plane. Where? Anne later wrote, "Sleeping in the plane was not necessarily uncomfortable. There was plenty of room in the big baggage compartment, where, before we had the pontoon tanks, a two-hundred gallon gasoline tank had once fitted. The small door in the side of the ship, through which the baggage was passed, made a perfect window."

I imagined the shuffling that took place as they prepared their bed for the evening. Looking at the small plane, it is hard to see where two people fit in front of the cockpit. She admitted that she sometimes felt like the girl from *The Princess and the Pea*, as they lay on a pile of supplies: "Our equipment, neatly packed on the floor in layers according to degrees of softness, made a comfortable bed. Everything was used, even the oars of our rubber boat, the tool-kit, the cans of emergency food, and our canteens . . . We were careful to put the oars and the cans at the bottom. First, the oars; then, the tool-kit and spare parts of the engine, the cans of food, the bulky canvas bags of emergency equipment, the rubber boat, the tent roll, extra coils of rope; next, our parachute packs; then our blanket rolls of clothing; our two flying suits for a top mattress; and, lastly, the sleeping bag."

Planning Does Matter

In the end, as Charles Lindbergh knew well, weight and careful planning did matter. On their second world flight in the *Tingmissartoq*, the Lindberghs were in Bathurst (now Banjul), Gambia, preparing to fly across the South Atlantic to Brazil. On the first take-off attempt, Charles could not raise the plane off the water; it was overloaded. Thus started a process of Charles carefully unloading equipment and clothing, an extra fuel tank, and some extra food to get the plane into the air. "I began to realize more vividly than ever before what those lists of my husband meant; those impressive itemized pages. . . . It was quite different perusing the lists now, on the eve of a transoceanic flight, when tomorrow we might be depending on them for our lives."

In life, no matter how careful the planning, unexpected situations arise. One scenario that Charles had not planned for abruptly brought an end to their first flight in the *Tingmissartoq*. While in

Hankow (now Wuhan), China, on the Yangtze River, the Lindberghs had stored the plane on the British airplane carrier *Hermes* because they had not been able to find a safe place to dock due to the flooded river's swift currents. They had been busy assisting with flood relief efforts in the surrounding region and had made various flights to deliver medical help. The day before they were to leave the area, Charles and Anne were in the cockpit as the plane was being lowered from the ship to the river for one last flight. The balance shifted and suddenly one wing dipped into the water like a giant paddle. As the current took the plane, the cables went taut, and the plane threatened to flip over in the water. The Lindberghs had no choice but to jump into the water and swim to a waiting lifeboat. Anne later described what she saw as she looked back at the plane: "For one sickening moment I thought the *Sirius* [*Tingmissartoq*] was going to pieces before our eyes. It was in the grip of a mad force, tireless, unceasing, and irresistible, which would devour it as fire devours a frame house. All the infinite care that goes to make up a plane, the smooth fashioning of the wood for the wings, the delicate precision of the machinery for the engine; and all our work, the whole summer—everything was to be lost in a few seconds in the destruction of the *Sirius*. It was no more than a little match box crushed in a giant's hand." The plane was ultimately saved and shipped back to America for major repair, but the Lindberghs' travels were temporarily over.

In the days before the exhibition opened, I watched the collections staff install the artifacts. The fish hooks and crampons for climbing on ice went into a sack. The cans of food supplies went into one of the crates. One staff member placed a large funnel next to a black-and-white photo of Charles Lindbergh holding the funnel. Another person installed a white wool parka with the dark stripe into a case in front of a photo of Anne wearing the parka. And finally someone installed the life-size photo of the smiling Lindberghs walking side by side, one tall and lanky, the other short and petite, ready to embark on another adventure.

Today, the *Tingmissartoq* stands restored to its former glory in the new "Pioneers of Flight" exhibition. The dock next to it is filled with provisions representative of the attempted anticipation of all that was possible. It's a silent testament to Charles and Anne Lindbergh and their two incredible flights in the black-and-red plane. I never tire of watching visitors explore the collection of artifacts that Charles Lindbergh had the foresight to save. Perhaps he wanted future generations to know of his packing prowess.

17
PASSIONATE
PRETENDERS

> If you like history, you'll probably like reenacting—
> one thing to remember though, you *will* feel
> what it was like. In reenacting you will feel the
> dirt, the sweat, the wool clothing.
>
> —*Reenactor.net introduction page*

If you could gather seven presidents from American history together for an evening of conversation, whom would you select? One day I sat around a table with George Washington, Thomas Jefferson, Calvin Coolidge, John Adams, Abraham Lincoln, and Franklin Roosevelt. Oh, and James Madison showed up at some point. Talk about a surreal experience. This odd mix was not my choice. Staff at the National Museum of American History had hired these character actors to add excitement and educational value to the opening of an exhibition about the presidency. Each bore a striking resemblance to the popular images of his president and carefully tried to replicate that person's speech and mannerisms. I especially liked Calvin Coolidge, Silent Cal, though most visitors did not recognize him.

Of course, he didn't have much to say. They didn't wear nametags, but it probably would have been a good idea. Their presentations combined both structured monologues and unscripted interaction with visitors, though only a few of them were comfortable with the latter. During a break in the day's festivities, I sat down at a table in the green room and started talking to Washington and Jefferson. Suddenly one by one, the others joined us and thus, I found myself surrounded. They chatted about life as a presidential actor—it was a job for them. Each had his own story about how he became involved in this rarest of professions.

One or two worked at museums, but most were independent contractors, traveling around the country to share their passion for history with others. The man who portrayed Thomas Jefferson works at Colonial Williamsburg and our paths have crossed several times. He has devoted his career to learning as much as he can about our third president. A trained actor, he approached staff at Williamsburg one day to see if they wanted a Jefferson to interact with visitors to the restored town. He's been at it for many years and has traveled the country as Jefferson, red hair pulled back in a queue. He was Jefferson, the Virginia governor, holding a press conference in Williamsburg, and Jefferson, the U.S. president, talking with Napoleon about the Louisiana Purchase in St. Louis. I organized a national teacher conference during the Lewis and Clark bicentennial and Colonial Williamsburg, one of the sponsors, sent Thomas Jefferson and Napoleon from their cast of characters. Although these two men never met in history, the resulting discussion about the Louisiana Purchase proved highly thought provoking.

My Brush with Reenacting

A variety of history museums utilize theater to enliven historical topics and touch visitors' emotions. Effective theater draws the audience into another time. The closest I ever came to reenacting a historical event occurred during the run of a special exhibition at the National Portrait Gallery focused on the life of noted orator, abolitionist, and former slave Frederick Douglass. Several years into the Civil War, the Lincoln administration finally approved the recruitment of black regiments. Douglass traveled throughout the North leading the effort to fill the ranks of the all-black 54th Massachusetts Regiment. Portrait Gallery staff decided to reenact a recruitment rally as an educational program in support of the exhibition. The event portrayed a "mass meeting of colored people" that took place on July 6, 1863, in Philadelphia's National Hall. Over five thousand people had gathered that day to hear powerful speeches and stirring music. Our event was no different, minus a few thousand in the audience. I donned nineteenth-century attire and stood out on the sidewalk with a sign to recruit an audience. The reenactors who portray the valiant men of the 54th Massachusetts, made famous in the movie *Glory*, are based in the Washington DC area and agreed to participate. Held in the historic Great Hall of the Portrait Gallery, the rally transported the audience back to the Civil War era through the patriotic music of a fife and drum corps and a series of rousing speeches culminating with a brilliant oration by an actor portraying Frederick Douglass.

Afterward, a long line of fresh recruits of all sizes and colors waited to sign the register to become honorary members of the 54th. I can't remember how many modern-day troops we added that day, but images from *Glory* played in my mind as I considered the sacrifice paid by the real heroes of the 54th. Though nearly 44 percent of the regiment were killed leading the bloody assault of Fort Wagner near Charleston, South Carolina, the courage of that and other units ultimately inspired the enlistment of over 186,000 black soldiers in the Union army. By August 1863, Douglass had resigned from his role as recruiter because he could no longer encourage enlistment in the face of continuing unequal treatment of black soldiers in the Union army.

The men of the 54th reenactment unit added a great deal of energy and drama to the Portrait Gallery program. However, generally, history professionals maintain a degree of suspicion regarding "history reenactors," the nonprofessionals who dress up in period clothing and seek to "experience history." Reenactors spend long weekends in the field to gain some small perspective on life in the past. While many thrill to the pulse-racing moments in battle reenactments, the majority pursue the hobby out of an honest passion to share history with the public. Their backgrounds vary greatly. Some are lured to the hobby in their retirement years, often skewing the average age higher than would be historically accurate. Younger men and women are busy with work and family obligations and have less leisure time for such hobbies. The Lewis and Clark reenactment groups I know contain many members who are well past the age of eighteen to thirty-four years of the young men who comprised the actual Corps of Discovery. It always strikes me as incongruent that audiences see these older men and think they represent the ages of the historical men. Alas, there are limits to historical accuracy.

Civil War reenactors are perhaps most familiar to the general public, but I've come into contact with almost every kind of reenactor, some not even human. Once my cousin and I attended a dog show at Oatlands Plantation near Leesburg, Virginia. A woman with a huge black Newfoundland stood nearby and I went over to pet the dog. I casually mentioned to the woman that Meriwether Lewis had taken his Newfoundland, Seaman, along on the expedition. "I know," she said nonchalantly. "In fact, Alfie here portrays Seaman in a Lewis and Clark reenactment group out of Harpers Ferry." A dog reenactor—of course, it made sense. Every Lewis and Clark group needs a Seaman. Not only that, they would be smart to have a backup. During the official reenactment voyage for the bicentennial in 2004, the dog portraying Seaman died unexpectedly, much to the sadness of the reenactors and the dog's owner, who portrayed Meriwether Lewis.

Reenactors choose their hobby for many reasons. Most have a burning desire to step back in time and to imagine a different way of life. They are willing to spend thousands of dollars on uniforms and equipment and endure weekends away from family. While many professional historians raise their eyebrows at the efforts of reenactors, when a national anniversary like the Lewis and Clark expedition rolls around, these groups usually receive invitations to official events and play key roles in the commemorations. The 200th anniversary of the Battle of Yorktown in 1981, the culmination of the nation's bicentennial celebration, included British, French, and American encampments. The reenactment of the surrender featured a grand parade where unit after unit marched in review past President Reagan and the President of France François Mitterrand.

A Critical Look at Living History

While in graduate school, I decided to take a critical look at what is called living history, the interpretive approach broadly defined by Jay Anderson as "simulation of life in another time with the purpose being research, interpretation, play or all three." I visited a Civil War encampment held each fall on the front lawn of the Lancaster County (PA) Historical Society. The event featured local reenactment groups such as the Independent Battery I, known as the Pennsylvania Light Artillery, the 30th Pennsylvania Infantry, Co. E, called the "Lancaster Guard," and the Patriot Daughters of Lancaster. The event organizers' goal was increased public awareness of the society and its programs, though another goal was educating the audience about local history. The encampment demonstrated the reality of life in a Union army camp. Visitors could watch a laundress washing clothes, soldiers cooking over a fire or playing cards, a chaplain working on a sermon, women camp followers sewing, and soldiers drilling. The event included music demonstrations, a recruitment rally, concerts, medical demonstrations, a fashion show, church service, and rifle competitions.

With my grad student's critical eye, I tested the encampment against a basic rubric constructed by living history proponent and museum professional John Fortier. He wrote that to qualify as living history, historical simulation "must be accompanied by a serious and active attempt to understand and empathize with the subject. . . . What separates living history from play acting . . . is whether those involved are doing their best to understand and explain." To Fortier quality living history efforts must feature passionate presenters who speak from their experiences as reenactors and care deeply about historical accuracy and historical context. Many Civil War reenactors don't speak in first person or portray a specific historical character. But their units expect them to know the history of the unit and the broader context of the era. Through participation in various events, reenactors gain experience that gives them a certain validity with the public. People ask them what it is like to sleep outside in a tent, to eat nineteenth-century-style food, and to face the "enemy" in battle reenactment. One reenactor told me that he learns from reenacting what the history books cannot teach. He learned the hard way how hot a canteen can become when left in the direct sun on a steamy July day—the water in it can burn the mouth.

Since reenacting is primarily a hobby, no governing body oversees it. Therefore, the question of historical accuracy is valid. Who ensures accuracy? Who defines accuracy? In his fascinating book *Confederates in the Attic*, Tony Horwitz delves into the world of some hardcore Civil War reenactors. One of the main characters in the book is known for his excellent skill at imitating a bloated battlefield corpse. He becomes the author's guide through the culture of reenactors, coaching Horwitz as he spends time in the field with a Virginia Civil War unit. Horwitz describes the quest for historical accuracy and wonders at the passion of this hardcore unit. Some reenactors go to great lengths to ensure accuracy—such as soaking uniform buttons in urine to get the correct patina—which most people would call obsessive attention to period detail. Even the word "reenactor" is distasteful to these hardcores. Horwitz quotes one person saying, "We're living historians, or historical interpreters if you like." Other reenactors are not as concerned with accuracy and are willing to make modern accommodations for comfort or convenience. "Farb," a universal term in the reenactor community, is the strongest of insults used for those reenactment units that mix the present with the past and only pay loose attention to detail.

The Mother of All Civil War Reenactments

I had worked in the history field for many years before I witnessed the mother of all Civil War reenactments—Gettysburg. While entertaining friends from California and Missouri one July 4, I offered them a trip to Gettysburg. One of the premier Civil War events of the reenactment season, it takes place annually on the anniversary of the battle. Not one who relishes heat and humidity, I had avoided the event in the past. But curiosity and the desire to be a good host got the best of me. We drove from Lancaster, Pennsylvania, west through rolling countryside and villages, to a dry dusty field on the outskirts of the small town of Gettysburg. The National Park Service does not permit reenactments on the battlefield's sacred ground, so organizers rent a local farm. The weather forecasters promised low humidity for the day, though we prepared to wilt in the heat.

A small village of white tents filled with both reenactors and goods for sale stood at the edge of a large field. Each day's main event was a full-scale battle reenactment. That day's featured battle was Little Roundtop, scheduled to take place, ironically, on relatively flat land. We joined several thousand people of all ages sitting on blankets and in lawn chairs around the roped-off area. Growing up nearby, I had taken many school field trips to Gettysburg and always struggled to imagine the fierce fighting and deafening noise of a Civil War battle while looking at the peaceful grassy fields. Aside from a skirmish or two, I had never seen reenactor armies clashing in battle. I wasn't sure what to expect. Once the fighting began, it was easy for my imagination to get lost in the sights, smells, and sounds of battle with cannons roaring and men shouting. Over the deafening boom of the cannon, an announcer tried to read a narration and provide explanation. Like a sports announcer calling the game, he made a valiant attempt to help the crowd focus on certain actions on the field.

I could stomach the incongruity of an announcer at a Civil War battle, but the Confederate charge of the flat hill was more than I could take. The disconnect brought my reverie to a quick end. Could they not find a field with a steeper slope? If I was the director . . . I soon found myself looking at the battle with an organizer's eye, trying to determine which of the soldiers would "die." How did they know when to drop dead? I assumed a director somewhere had choreographed the event and was aiming for accuracy, so as the narrator described the various movements, I found myself again critiquing the effort. The crowds seemed to be engaged in the action and I wondered what they were learning. What draws people to a battle reenactment? How are they connecting to history? I briefly recalled those morbidly curious Washingtonians who took picnic lunches to watch the First Battle of Bull Run in 1861 and were surprised to find themselves caught in the action and fleeing back to the safety of Washington.

Besides the battle reenactment, the day's schedule included concerts, lectures, demonstrations, tours of camp, and church services. The most captivating of the camp demonstrations occurred in the hospital tent. Immediately after the battle, the hospital staff carried in a wounded soldier. His leg was bleeding profusely and the doctor went to work. As he worked, he explained what he was doing to the crowd gathered round. He described the nature of the wound and his options as a surgeon based on the medical knowledge in that time period and the available medication. He decided that he needed to amputate, so to the horror of the crowd, he took out his dirty saw and began sawing. As the blood spurted, his saw stopped briefly at what sounded like a bone. He kept sawing. The leg dropped off, with blood gushing and appropriate screaming from the soldier. The action had a grand effect on the crowd, which gasped and stood riveted. As the program wrapped up and the soldier stood up all in one piece, I decided that including a little blood and gore proved an effective way to teach history. I had no way to measure my conclusion other than to cite a crowd giving its full attention to someone in a bloody white apron. Perhaps it was over-the-top on gore, but also most likely a moment that would linger long in the audience's memories.

During the course of the day, as I mingled with the reenactors, I spotted a man who looked like General Ulysses S. Grant. Yet, as any history student knows, Grant was far from Gettysburg during the battle. He was busy in Vicksburg, Mississippi, putting the squeeze on the Confederate forces there and finishing off his siege, culminating with Vicksburg's surrender the day after Gettysburg. I said, "Hello, General Grant." He nodded. "You aren't supposed to be here," I whispered.

"I'm not here," he replied with a slight grin and a wink. What would the hardcore reenactors think of that?

The mystery of how reenactors in battle decide to die was solved when I talked to one of them around the time of the 150th reenactment of the Battle of Manassas. He told me no one wants to die immediately since the thrill is in the battle movement, not lying still in the hot sun. Some event organizers hand out cards to each side that are color coded to match the percentage of casualties from that particular engagement. If you draw the colored card, you must die. When it's your time, there are other considerations. You obviously want to keel over after a gunshot. You want to avoid manure piles, ant hills, and other potentially unpleasant spots. If it's a hot day, you try to maneuver so that you find a shady spot (apparently a disproportionate number of reenactors die in the shade) or at minimum cock your hat so it shields your face. If you're hardcore, you might die on your stomach so the audience can't see you breathing. You can take a nap if you're comfortable, and hope you don't get stepped on. Some men have snuck cameras onto the battlefield, and the dead have been known to snap photos from their unique position. Talk about farby!

Surrounded by Germans

"Calling all Germans. We need you for the battle."

The announcement blasted over the loudspeaker just as a P-51 flew overhead. I was baking my brains in the scorching sun at an air show. Directly behind me was a camp of German soldiers. For many years my experience with reenactors was limited to the Civil War period and earlier. One year, however, my Uncle Paul, a World War II veteran, invited me to an extravaganza in Reading, Pennsylvania. The massive annual event is the largest World War II encampment and air show in the United States, filling several acres on the grounds of the local airport. Row after row of tents in all shapes and sizes represented both the European and Pacific theaters—Russian, Canadian, British, and even Polish. A recreated French village stood close to displays about the home front, a victory garden, and a canteen. The schedule included concerts, lectures, reenacted radio shows, and simulated skirmishes, and the day ended with a World War II–era concert and dance. Periodically throughout the day various motorcades drove by—FDR and Eleanor Roosevelt waving from one, Generals Patton or MacArthur saluting from another. Bob Hope's show proved popular, as were the Andrews sisters.

Many of the special guests had been directly involved in the war efforts, including one of Germany's most respected Luftwaffe fighter pilots, a crew member from the *Enola Gay*, a woman from the Army Nursing Corps, and Tuskegee Airmen from the Philadelphia chapter. The Band of Brothers guys from the 101st Airborne also drew many fans.

During a break in the airshow, the "battle" commenced. Sixty or so Americans in troop transports far outnumbered the sad assortment of about twenty-five German foot soldiers. Slowly the two sides crept toward each other and with a shot the fighting began, gun smoke filling the heavy air. After at least fifty shots, the first casualty fell.

"It's about time someone falls," my cousin muttered. "Not exactly crack shots, are they?"

Soon men on both sides were flinging their bodies to the ground in dramatic gestures. The medics raced to the wounded with a stretcher. The entire episode was over in about fifteen minutes. The remaining Germans surrendered and were taken off the field. Where was the educational value? Perhaps this battle was for the reenactors, to give them battlefield experience.

One question puzzled me the entire day and I finally decided to seek some answers. I marched over to the German camp. The first lone soldier I came across, a member of the Grossdeutschland Division, looked reasonably harmless.

"What made you decide to join a German regiment?" I asked, trying to keep an even tone to my voice.

"Most of us have German heritage, and it's an opportunity to show that the common German soldier was just following orders like the common American soldier. There was little difference." He continued, "Now some other units portray ss soldiers and those are controversial, as you can imagine. They receive their share of conflict and are not invited to some events."

Hmm. I came across a young man adjusting his uniform. I noticed the ss insignia at his collar covered with a piece of black tape. He explained that the event requires them to cover the offensive symbol. He told me of a colleague who wore his uniform to an event near Philadelphia and got beaten up. The young soldier, also of German heritage, described his fascination with German army equipment as a child. When he found out my uncle was a veteran, he thanked him for his service. Turned out he was a reservist in real life and casually said he was headed to Afghanistan in two days on his first tour of duty. He would be driving tanks. We returned the thanks and continued on our way.

I approached a cook in the mess tent of yet another German camp. He was stirring a soup that smelled wonderful. While my uncle asked him about his cooking process and equipment, I looked at another soldier a few feet away. This time I asked if most of the soldiers in his company had German heritage. He answered with a clipped accent—whoa, I'd found a genuine German. In the sea of German impostors, the fact that a German native was playing a German soldier made me a bit uncomfortable. I didn't bother to ask him why he is a reenactor. As we walked through the rest of the camp, we passed an array of men in their German uniforms. One had a neck filled with tattoos, including a swastika. Though I wanted to ask about historical accuracy in regards to tattoos, I didn't really feel like talking with him. After twelve hours in the broiling sun, my curiosity was sated.

I couldn't help but compare the event to Gettysburg. The World War II event was different in that the memory is still fresh. A nostalgic tone permeated the air. With the heroes signing books in a far tent and gray-haired vets moving slowly through the camps, the past collided with the present in an odd way. Uncle Paul and several of his friends who came along that day, all veterans of World War II, wore their military hats and emblems proudly. As we made our way through the encampments, I was touched to see the reenactors treat them like royalty. They were the living embodiment of what the reenactors sought to simulate and were recognized as primary sources. The immersive environment awakened memories of long ago and my uncle began telling stories.

Reenacting Redcoats

One Sunday on the way to church I noticed some Redcoats getting out of several cars parked at the side of the road. "Only in Virginia," I thought, where history seems to permeate every foot of ground. I made a mental note, and sure enough several hours later when I passed again, two dozen or so British Redcoats had set up camp next to several Hessians and perhaps four dozen Continental soldiers. The smell of campfires and stew wafted in the air: a Revolutionary War encampment had suddenly materialized. Every year the City of Alexandria celebrates George Washington's birthday with this nod to the eighteenth century held, ironically, at Fort Ward, a park on the site of a *Civil War* fort.

I seized the opportunity to talk with the British soldiers, members of the 4th Company Brigade of Guards, historically based in London, but in reality Americans living in northern Virginia and Charlotte, North Carolina. What motivates a reenactor to portray the enemy? "Well," admitted one, "some of us like being the bad guys." Another insisted that in the hierarchy of reenacting, people portraying the Revolutionary War period are generally more authentic because it is harder to obtain uniforms, they must be hand-sewn, whereas Civil War uniforms come off the rack. This soldier went so far as to say that those who portray Redcoats are more serious about historical accuracy. And they are mostly Anglophiles—no surprise there. He said the Hessian guys are interested in German history and some like to practice their language skills. One claimed his friend portrays a Hessian because he likes the fancy green uniforms. "The poseur," he muttered. Plus, ultimately, if you want to reenact a skirmish or battle, you need two sides. Good point.

I remain fascinated with living history and sometimes wonder how the hobby never managed to lure me into its grip. The passion of these peculiar folks is genuine and I feel obligated to applaud any desire to teach history. In some ways, though, it does appear as adult dress-up and an attempt to escape modernity. Whether practiced as an interpretive technique at a legitimate historic site or as a group of reenactors having some weekend fun, living history will always have its share of critics. I will most likely find myself drawn to another encampment or reenactment at some point, and I guess as long as there aren't too many farbs present, I will play along and pretend I have traveled to another time.

EPILOGUE

History, by apprising [the people] of the past,
will enable them to judge of the future.

—*Thomas Jefferson*

This was not your normal elevator ride. Crammed in with seven of my Air and Space Museum colleagues and two others, we rose to 195 feet. The doors opened to warm sunshine, a slight breeze, and a wide panorama of the Atlantic Ocean, waves crashing on the long, narrow stretch of Cape Canaveral beach below. Directly ahead, the bridge leading to the entry hatch of the space shuttle *Atlantis* beckoned us. We stood on the gantry of launch pad 39A, stunned into silence and in awe of the huge object before us. We were about to take the same walk as the shuttle astronauts. With a rapidly beating heart, I crossed the bridge to the "white room," the small compartment on the gantry that fits around the spacecraft, providing a vestibule from which the astronauts enter the craft. I kneeled next to the entry hatch and looked in. As I turned my head I could see the cockpit.

When I began my journey into history, I would never have expected to have this opportunity to get up close and personal with a space shuttle. The first reusable shuttle had launched into the blue Florida sky over the Kennedy Space Center complex twenty-seven years earlier, but now the shuttle era was quickly coming to an end. Only eleven or so missions remained. The National Air and Space Museum had secured funding to develop an exhibition about the history of the shuttle era and the international space station. To my historian's sensibilities the topic hardly seemed history, but current events. A section of this exhibition, unlike others I'd worked on, would attempt to look into the future, a challenge for anyone but especially for historians. As our small group stood in wonder—the shuttle nose rising high above our heads, encased in a protective stabilizing framework—we each recognized that the task ahead of us would be difficult. How would we convey to millions of people the challenges of human space travel? To many Americans the shuttle flights had become routine—despite the tragedies of *Challenger* and *Columbia*. Somehow space missions no longer seemed difficult and dangerous. The shuttle era was coming to an end, and both the glories and the tragedies it held were already written in the history books.

My professional history career, which started in eighteenth-century Williamsburg, had now led me to the brink of the future. Truth be told, I never had much interest in human space exploration. But my visit to the launch pad that day began a personal transformation. I could not stand atop the launch tower, under the mammoth shuttle engines, or next to the massive fuel tank without feeling a sense of total amazement at the engineering feat that they represented. While the astronauts received much of the glory, behind every astronaut stood thousands of people who worked to ensure a safe mission, every one with a story to tell.

History is filled with spectacular triumphs and failures. We visited launch complex 5/6 where Alan Shepard in his *Freedom 7* became the first American in space. The control room is designed to look much like it did on that historic day in 1961, cigarette butts in the ashtrays, the red launch button tempting me to press it. We also visited pad 34 where America lost its first astronauts in the *Apollo 1* tragedy. Three white stone benches stand in isolation, each inscribed with a name. Those astronauts sacrificed their lives for the dream of space exploration.

Why should people care about the past? Because our future depends on how well we learn its lessons. Thomas Jefferson was right, history's power lies in the fact that it informs the future. I love history because it incites my imagination and offers endless stories of real people who faced tough challenges. But whether slaves debating the meaning of freedom, Lewis and Clark encountering unfamiliar native customs, or John Brown leading deadly protests, the stories don't mean much unless I apply them to my own experiences and the world around me. History is a discipline that helps us understand ourselves and our world. It reminds us that we each have the power, great or small, for better or worse, to shape the future.

ACKNOWLEDGMENTS

I would like to thank the following people, who all contributed to this book in some way.

No one deserves my gratitude more than my parents, Orie and Kathryn Grove, who took me to visit many historical sites in my childhood and supported my budding interest in history in numerous ways. They encouraged me to pursue my dreams and never questioned how a person can earn a living in "history."

My cousin Nancy Sebastian Meyer blazed the publishing trail in our family and provided invaluable encouragement, guidance, and technical support. She offered critical review of the entire manuscript.

Writers 2.0—my writers group: Joanne Redmond Beckham, Catherine and David Swinson, Chris Joyce, and Dave Todaro. Their constant encouragement and their review of many chapters at the beginning kept me writing.

My Lewis and Clark colleagues Carolyn Gilman, Jeff Meyer, and Diane Mallow made that project the most fun I've ever had at work. Their professionalism combined with a tireless sense of humor resulted in an exhibition and Web site that I feel is one of my greatest achievements.

I will be forever indebted to Ruth Hill, Nancy McCoy, and Maureen Kerr, my three supervisors during my Smithsonian years. They all took a chance with hiring me, assigned me interesting projects, and taught me much about the museum field. My time as program manager of the Hands On History Room, alongside my HOHR colleague Heather Paisley-Jones and the many dedicated volunteers who staffed the space, challenged me to think about history in new ways and gave me a perfect opportunity to observe people interacting with the past.

Roy Underhill and Conny Graft helped make my short summer in Williamsburg a pivotal point in my career; Conny, Mark Howell, and Bill Peterson all graciously shared their experiences for this book.

Bob Sutton, Chief Historian of the National Park Service, first taught me the history of the American West and encouraged me to pursue Lewis and Clark, one of the best decisions I ever made.

Andy Gulliford led my first Lewis and Clark tour and gave me crucial motivation at the right time in my career. We endured the water battle on the Missouri together and discussed public history on a walk down the empty streets of Three Forks, Montana, and the horseback ride up to the Smoking Place.

Special thanks to Barbara Decker, who provided a critical early review of my manuscript and much encouragement.

My St. Louis friends Petra Blum, Jon Marsh, and Sara Swinson first encouraged me to write my stories. Their initial interest showed me that perhaps the adventures would resonate with a wider audience. In many ways this book exists because of them.

My cousin Earl Grove loaned me a computer at a crucial stage of writing. My cousin Michael Lowery created the illustrations. Jeremiah Coder provided legal counsel. Kevin Mitchell and Siobhan Smith read early versions of the manuscript. The following people all reviewed various chapters and provided critical feedback: Bob Beatty, Tricia Brooks, Leni Buff, Carolyn Gilman, Conny Graft, Ruth Hill, Andrea Lowther, Nancy McCoy, Howard Morrison, and David Romanowski.

Jay Blossom, Sandor Der, Dale and Susan Hoffmeyer, Hunter

Irvine, and Paul and Jean Sebastian provided constant encouragement over many years.

Thanks to my editor, Bridget Barry, for taking a chance on this book and the staff of the University of Nebraska Press, who embraced this project and guided it to completion.

Two organizations that I've supported over the years deserve my thanks as well: the American Association for State and Local History (AASLH) strives to foster excellence among its broad membership. Through my involvement with AASLH I've met wonderful people who have stretched my thinking about history. The National History Day organization, by teaching critical thinking skills through original research, is a leader in history education for students across the country. They are developing the history leaders of tomorrow and my involvement with their program is a continuing source of inspiration.

NOTES

Introduction

xi   **"for the true student of history"**: John F. Kennedy, "JFK On Our Nation's Memory," *American Heritage* (reprinted Winter 2010), 16. In 1962 at the request of the editors of *American Heritage*, President Kennedy wrote an essay about the importance of history.

1. Why History?

3   **"Awaken people's curiosity"**: Widely attributed to Anatole France.

8   **"History does not refer merely"**: Eric Foner, *Who Owns History? Rethinking the Past in a Changing World* (New York: Hill and Wang, 2002), ix.

8   **"There is little that is more important"**: Kennedy, "JFK On Our Nation's Memory," 16.

2. Stepping Back in Time, Almost

12   **"The teaching approach"**: Warren Leon and Margaret Piatt, "Living-History Museums," in *History Museums in the United States* (Urbana: University of Illinois Press, 1989), 64.

15   **Historian Freeman Tilden wrote**: Freeman Tilden, *Interpreting Our Heritage*, 4th ed. (Chapel Hill: University of North Carolina Press, 2008).

20   **"The past is never dead"**: William Faulkner, *Requiem for a Nun* (New York: Random House, 1951), act 1, scene 3.

3. Challenging History

24   **"[T]hat noblest of Washington buildings"**: Charles J. Robertson, *Temple of Invention* (London: Scala Publishers, 2006), 10. Quotations about the National Portrait Gallery in this chapter are all taken from this source.

29   **John Brown's raid provided**: The "Trial of John Brown" program was presented by the National Portrait Gallery Education Department from 1972 to 2000.

31   **"Americans do not deliberate"**: Dennis Frye, Chief Historian, Harpers Ferry National Park, in "Day of Reckoning," *Smithsonian*, October 2009, 62.

32   **In the decades after the raid**: Teresa S. Moyer and Paul A. Shackel, *The Making of Harpers Ferry National Historical Park* (Lanham MD: Altamira Press, 2008), is the main source for the history of John Brown's fort.

4. The Everest of Museums

41   **"It was their duty"**: Nina Burleigh, *The Stranger and the Statesman* (New York: William Morrow, 2003), 192. John Quincy Adams quotes in this chapter are taken from this source as well. Another excellent source for the James Smithson story is Heather Ewing, *The Lost World of James Smithson* (New York: Bloomsburg, 2007).

44   **Hands On History Room**: The HOHR opened in November 1985 as part the exhibition "Life After the Revolution." Staff expanded the room to two thousand square feet in the early 1990s and it closed for good in August 2004.

5. Conquering the High Wheeler

49   **Epigraph**: Mark Twain's essay about his experience riding a high wheeler, titled "Taming the Bicycle," is widely available online.

55   **When the solitary wayfarer**: Robert A Smith, *The Social History of the Bicycle* (Winter Park FL: American Heritage Press, 1972), foreword.

55   **"When a man is riding"**: Seamus McGonagle, *The Bicycle in Love, War and Literature* (New York: A. S. Barnes, 1969), 32.

57   **"a physician who uses"**: Thomas Stevens, *Around the World on a Penny-Farthing* (1888; repr., London: Arrow Books, 1991), 34.

57   "The greatest drawback": Stevens, *Around the World*, 35.

57   "I consider it a lucky": Stevens, *Around the World*, 32.

6. Does This Make Cotton or Gin?

64   **John Earl Little of New Albany:** Reminiscences of John Earl Little collected by Christina M. Little, in "Transcripts," Interactive History Project, Palo Alto College, http://pacweb.alamo.edu/interactivehistory/ projects/people/categories/VanishingOccupations/Little-Little/Oral HistoryTemplate.html#Trans (accessed July 20, 2013).

64   **One morning, long before:** Solomon Northup, *Twelve Years a Slave: Narrative of Solomon Northup*, Documenting the American South (Auburn: Derby and Miller, 1853), 178–79, digitized at http://docsouth.unc.edu/ fpn/northup/northup.html.

66   **One day a new story:** A summary of Angela Lakwete's research can be found in Angela Lakwete, *Inventing the Cotton Gin: Machine and Myth in Antebellum America* (Baltimore: Johns Hopkins University Press, 2005).

69   **"The cotton gin cranked":** Eli Whitney to Thomas Jefferson, Petition for a Patent, 20 June, 1793, in Lakwete, *Inventing the Cotton Gin*, 200, n. 1.

69   **"it is entirely new":** Whitney to Jefferson, Petition for a Patent.

70   **But it comes as no surprise:** Mrs. Greene's contribution mentioned in Lakwete, *Inventing the Cotton Gin*, 184.

70   **"It has been my endeavor":** Eli Whitney to Thomas Jefferson, 15 October 1793, in Lakwete, *Inventing the Cotton Gin*, 200, n. 3.

70   **"The State of Virginia":** Thomas Jefferson to Eli Whitney, Jr., 16 November 1793, Eli Whitney Papers, Manuscripts and Archives, Yale University Library.

71   **"only after two decades":** Angela Lakwete, "Roller and Saw Cotton Gin Carts Training Manual" (unpublished manuscript, National Museum of American History), 32.

7. Mary, Not Betsy

73   **Epigraph:** You can view the earliest known version of the Francis Scott Key's manuscript of the song lyrics at http://amhistory.si.edu/starspangled banner/the-lyrics.aspx (accessed August 20, 2013).

75   **thirty-by-thirty-four-foot flag:** The original flag was thirty by forty-two

feet, but by the time it came to the Smithsonian in 1907 it was missing eight feet of material from the fly end because several owners had given fragments of the flag to worthy recipients as mementos. One star is also missing for the same reason. See Lonn Taylor, *The Star-Spangled Banner: The Flag That Inspired the National Anthem* (New York: Harry N. Abrams, 2000), 52–53.

77   **Rarely is an object**: Taylor, *The Star-Spangled Banner*.

77   **Yet the more I read**: A helpful source for this chapter was Walter Lord, *The Dawn's Early Light* (New York: W. W. Norton, 1972).

83   **"Ah, Mr. Skinner, after"**: Lord, *Dawn's Early Light*, 256.

84   **Mary Pickersgill's American flag**: Historians are not sure if it was the large garrison flag (the Star-Spangled Banner) or the smaller storm flag, both sewn by Mary Pickersgill. See note in Lord, *Dawn's Early Light*, 365.

84   **"The song, I know"**: Quoted in Harold I. Lessem and George C. Mac-Kenzie, *Fort McHenry National Monument and Historic Shrine, Maryland* (Washington DC: National Park Service, 1954, 1961), http://www.nps.gov/history/history/online_books/hh/5/hh5h.htm (accessed July 20, 2013).

86   **"As the last vessel"**: Taylor, *The Star-Spangled Banner*, 21.

8. That Strange Creature the Mule

Two helpful sources for this chapter were Janet Vorwald Dohner, *The Encyclopedia of Historic and Endangered Livestock and Poultry Breeds* (New Haven: Yale University Press, 2001), and Alan and Donna Jean Fusonie, *G W Pioneer Farmer* (Alexandria VA: Mount Vernon Ladies Association, 1998).

91   **"I have my hopes"**: George Washington to William Fitzhugh, May 15, 1786, quoted in note 2, "To George Washington from Samuel Vaughan, 4 November 1788," Founders Online, http://founders.archives.gov/documents/Washington/05-01-02-0071#GEWN-05-01-02-0071-fn-0002 (accessed July 21, 2013).

91   **"I have a prospect"**: "From George Washington to Arthur Young, December 4, 1788," Founders Online, http://founders.archives.gov/documents/Washington/05-01-02-0120 (accessed July 21, 2013).

93   **According to scholar Donald Kraybill**: Donald Kraybill, *The Riddle of Amish Culture* (Baltimore: Johns Hopkins University Press, 1989).

9. When Houses Talk

106 **"Nothing you ever read"**: Sarah Orne Jewett to Sarah Wyman Whitman, July 30, 1892 (Houghton Library, Harvard University), in Paula Blanchard, *Sarah Orne Jewett: Her World and Her Work* (New York: Perseus Books, 1994), 254.

106 **"[T]he beliefs of those"**: John Herbst, "Historic Houses," in *History Museums in the United States* (Urbana: University of Illinois Press, 1989), 100.

109 **"[G]entlemen of fortune were"**: Marian Page, *Historic Houses Restored and Preserved* (New York: Whitney Library of Design, 1976), 34.

10. Water Battle on the Missouri

117 **"The charge of the expedition"**: Meriwether Lewis to Lucy Marks, July 2, 1803, Missouri Historical Society Archives, St. Louis MO.

119 **"the grandest sight"**: Source for all Lewis and Clark journal quotations is Bernard DeVoto, ed., *The Journals of Lewis and Clark* (New York: Houghton Mifflin, 1981). In most cases I have used modern spellings for clarity.

11. You Can't Write My History

130 **"writingest explorers of their time"**: Donald Jackson, ed., *Letters of the Lewis and Clark Expedition* (Urbana: University of Illinois Press, 1978), vii.

131 **"When the dried meat"**: Ella Clark, *Indian Legends from the Northern Rockies* (Norman OK: University of Oklahoma Press, 1966), 130–31.

131 **"Well if they bring"**: Allen Pinkham, as told to author, St. Louis MO, December 2002.

133 **"the pipe ritual aimed"**: James Ronda, "The Objects of Our Journey," in Carolyn Gilman, *Lewis and Clark: Across the Divide* (Washington DC: Smithsonian Institution Press, 2003), 36–37.

136 **Who owns history?**: Foner, *Who Owns History*, xix.

140 **"Whereas Euro-American society trusts"**: Gilman, *Lewis and Clark*, 329.

12. A Grizzly in the Mail

147 **"The process of tracing"**: Gilman, *Lewis and Clark*, 336.

148 **According to scientist Daniel Botkin**: Daniel Botkin, *Our Natural History: The Lessons of Lewis and Clark* (New York: G. P. Putnam's Sons, 1995).

149 **Another item, quite ordinary**: The story of the corn mill and other stories from the exhibition are told in *Lewis and Clark: Across the Divide*, the exhibition catalog for "Lewis & Clark: The National Bicentennial Exhibition."

157 **"[h]istory always has been"**: Foner, *Who Owns History*, xvii.

13. Tracking the Buffalo

159 **"As we were riding"**: John C. Frémont, *The Exploring Expedition to the Rocky Mountains* (Washington DC: Smithsonian Institution Press, 1988), 23.

162 **"Tracking the Buffalo"**: The Web activity can be found online, at http://americanhistory.si.edu/buffalo/ (accessed August 26, 2013).

162 **"The buffalo didn't belong"**: Geoffrey C. Ward, *The West: An Illustrated History* (New York: Little, Brown, 1996), 263.

162 **That the extermination of**: Dale F. Lott, *American Bison: A Natural History* (Berkeley: University of California Press, 2002).

163 **"These men [buffalo hunters]"**: This quote is widely attributed to General Philip Sheridan, but I could not locate the original source.

163 **"Everything the Kiowas"**: Alice Marriott and Carol K. Rachlin, *American Indian Mythologies* (New York: Harper & Row, 1968).

163 **"We runners [hunters] served"**: *The West: An Illustrated History*, 283–84.

165 **"I like them because"**: Padgett Powell, "I Am Suspicious of a Soft Body," *Believer*, September 2006, http://www.believermag.com/issues/200609/?read=interview_powell (accessed July 21, 2013).

167 **"I have learned to respect"**: Max Harward, *Where the Buffalo Roam: Life on Antelope Island* (self-published, 1996), 58.

169 **"Plains Indians did not"**: Gilman, *Lewis and Clark*, 178.

169 **"The spirit of Tatanka"**: Gilman, *Lewis and Clark*, 179.

170 **"I never saw anyone"**: H. W. Brands, *T.R.: The Last Romantic* (New York: Basic Books, 1997), 158.

170 **"It was an event"**: Chief Luther Standing Bear, *My Indian Boyhood* (Lincoln: University of Nebraska Press, 1931), 177.

171 **"To reestablish healthy buffalo"**: Fred DuBray, in interview featured in the online version of "Lewis and Clark: The National Bicentennial Exhibition" (2003), http://lewisandclarkexhibit.org/cd_index_flash.html (accessed August 26, 2013).

14. The Cathedral and the Cemetery

179 **"I fear this report"**: William Clark to Jonathan Clark, October 28, 1809, in James Holmberg, ed. *Dear Brother: Letters of William Clark to Jonathan Clark* (New Haven CT: Yale University Press, 2002), 216–18.

15. We're Flying over Hell Stretch?

187 **"aviation and space flight"**: Tom D. Crouch, "Aerospace Museums: A Question of Balance," *Curator* 50, no. 1 (January 2007), accessed online.

187 **"For not a few visitors"**: Joseph J. Corn, *The Winged Gospel* (Baltimore: Johns Hopkins University Press, 2002), 142.

192 **"The route across"**: Bonny Farmer, "Flying the Hell Stretch," http://ww1.prweb.com/prfiles/2012/09/26/9947671/Flying%20the%20Hell%20Stretch.pdf (accessed January 11, 2013).

193 **Rivers perhaps are the**: Anne Morrow Lindbergh, *North to the Orient* (New York: Harcourt Brace, 1935), 112–13.

195 **"epitomized everything that was"**: Farmer, "Flying the Hell Stretch." Another good source for information about early airmail pilots is Barry Rosenberg and Catherine Macaulay, *Mavericks of the Sky* (New York: William Morrow, 2006).

195 **"I have received several"**: Superintendence D. B. Colyer to Bill Hopson, July 23, 1920, Record Group 28, Records of the Post Office Department, National Archives.

195 **Major newspapers across the country**: *Washington Post*, October 24, 1928; *New York Times*, October 22, 1928; *Los Angeles Times*, October 22, 1928.

196 **"So 'Hoppie,' Old Boy"**: Historian, U.S. Postal Service, "Airmail Pilot Bill Hopson," USPS.com (under "Postal People," "Other Personnel"), August 2005, http://about.usps.com/who-we-are/postal-history/airmail-pilot-bill-hopson.pdf (accessed July 27, 2013).

196 **"These young adventurers"**: *Los Angeles Times*, October 23, 1928.

16. How Lucky Was Lindy?

201 **"Every object to be"**: Lindbergh, *North to the Orient*, 10.

201 **"always packed up the"**: Lindbergh, *North to the Orient*, 109–10.

202 **"I would have been"**: A. Scott Berg, *Lindbergh* (New York: Berkley Books, 1998), 227. This is an excellent biography of Lindbergh.

208   "**Sleeping in the plane**": Lindbergh, *North to the Orient*, 95.

209   "**Our equipment, neatly packed**": Lindbergh, *North to the Orient*, 95.

209   "**I began to realize**": Anne Morrow Lindbergh, *Listen! The Wind* (New York: Harcourt Brace, 1938), 144–45.

210   "**For one sickening moment**": Lindbergh, *North to the Orient*, 130.

17. Passionate Pretenders

217   "**simulation of life in**": Jay Anderson, *The Living History Sourcebook* (Nashville: American Association for State and Local History, 1984), 460.

218   "**must be accompanied by**": John Fortier, "Dilemmas of Living History," in *Proceedings of the Annual Meeting, Vol. 10* (Washington DC: Association for Living Historical Farms and Agricultural Museums, 1989), 4–5.

218   **To Fortier quality living**: Fortier, "Dilemmas of Living History," 9.

218   **In his fascinating book**: Tony Horwitz, *Confederates in the Attic* (New York: Vintage Books, 1989).

Epilogue

227   **Epigraph**: Thomas Jefferson, *Notes on the State of Virginia* (1782). Many versions are widely available.